THE
INSPIRED LEADER

A REFERENCE GUIDE

JENN LOFGREN

The author of this book does not dispense medical advice or prescribe the use of any technique as a form of treatment for medical, emotional, or physical problems without the advice of a medical professional, either directly or indirectly. The intent of the author is to offer information in your quest in personal development. In the event you use any of the information in this book for yourself, which is your constitutional right, the author and publisher assume no responsibility for your actions.

Visit the Official Website at: https://incito.ca

Printed in the United States of America

First Printing: February 2022

Incito Executive & Leadership Development

ISBN-13: 978-0-578-36089-8

Incito Executive & Leadership Development books may be purchased for educational, business or sales promotional use. Special discounts are available on quantity purchases. For more information, please call or write.

Telephone: 403-922-2224; Email: inspire@incito.ca

For orders by U.S. trade bookstores and wholesalers, please contact Incito Executive & Leadership Development at the phone or email address listed above.

DISCLAIMER

The Publisher has strived to be as accurate and complete as possible in the creation of this book. This book is not intended for use as a source of financial, marketing or business advice. All readers are advised to seek services of competent professionals in the business leadership field.

Readers are cautioned to rely on their own judgment about their individual circumstances to act accordingly.

While all attempts have been made to verify information provided in this publication, the Publisher assumes no responsibility for errors, omissions, or contrary interpretation of the subject matter herein. Any perceived slights of specific persons, peoples, or organizations are unintentional. This book details the author's own personal experiences and opinions.

The author and publisher are providing this book and its contents on an "as is" basis and make no representations or warranties of any kind with respect to this book or its contents. The author and publisher disclaim all such representations and warranties, including for example warranties of merchantability and educational or medical advice for a particular purpose. In addition, the author and publisher do not represent or warrant that the information accessible via this book is accurate, complete or current.

Except as specifically stated in this book, neither the author or publisher, nor any authors, contributors, or other representatives will be liable for damages arising out of or in connection with the use of this book. This is a comprehensive limitation of liability that applies to all damages of any kind, including (without limitation) compensatory; direct, indirect or direct, indirect or consequential damages; loss of data, income or profit; loss of or damage to property and claims of third parties.

You understand that this book is not intended as a substitute for consultation with a licensed financial, legal or accounting professional. This book provides content related to business leadership topics. As such, use of this book implies your acceptance of this disclaimer.

TABLE OF CONTENTS

Foreword by David Irvine 1

Introduction 5

EMBRACING LEADERSHIP

Let Go Of What You 'Need to Know'......................................13

Questioning Your Leadership Ability?
Here's How To Cast Away The Doubt.....................................17

For Senior Executives, Personal Development Is
Professional Development...21

It's Lonely At The Top: Dealing With
Imposter Syndrome At The Executive Level............................27

Is Your Humility Hurting You? What Happens
When You Acknowledge Your Value 31

Stop Doing What You 'Should' Do And
Turn Your Thoughts Into Action..35

LEADERSHIP STYLE

Why You Can't Be Both A Leader And An Expert...........................43

What Type Of Leader Do You Want To Be? 47

The Approachable Leader: Adapting Your Style
To Work For Your Employees..53

Becoming A Magnetic Leader: How To Draw
The Potential From Your People..57

Developing Leadership Influence In Your Industry
And With Your Team 61

Four Skills You Need For Courageous Leadership 65

EMOTIONAL INTELLIGENCE

New Perspectives On Leadership Learned
From A 1,200-Pound Animal..73

Emotionally Intelligent Leaders Don't
Shut Off Their Emotions—They Manage Them 77

How Leaders Can Share Tough News Effectively
And With Empathy...81

The Port In The Storm: What Leaders Can Do
To Keep Calm In A Crisis..85

Managing Triggers Under Stress...89

How To Find Fulfillment As A Leader 93

BOUNDARIES & CHOICE

The Role That Boundaries Play In Leadership Growth........101

Is Your Open Door Policy Hurting You As A Leader? 105

Being A Likeable Leader Doesn't Mean
Being Liked All The Time...109

Rebuilding Your Authority When Your
Leadership Is Overstepped...113

Is It No Longer A Fit At Your Company?
Here's How To Move Forward 117

How Executives Should Be Spending Their Time............121

If There's Never Enough Time,
Time Management Isn't Your Real Problem.......................125

It Takes Courage For Leaders
To End Things When Necessary...129

ACCOUNTABILITY

Accountability And The Roles We All Play 137

What To Do When Getting
Circular Commitments From Your Team 141

Policies Vs. Guidelines: How To Set Clear Expectations 145

Not Getting The Results You Want
From Your Team? It Could Be You....................................149

How To Coach An 'Uncoachable' Employee 153

Tired Of Being "Monkey In The Middle"?
How To Help Your Team Win Their Own Battles 157

Tough Conversations And How Best To Approach Them.............161

How To Lead Through Big (And Small) Changes 167

RECHARGE

Unlock The Benefits Of Taking A Work Break 175

Leaders Are Allowed To Sleep Too: How To Stop
Suffering Through Sleepless Nights..................................179

How To Balance Work And Personal Obligations
Over The Holidays (And Year-Round)..............................183

Headed Back To Work After A Break?
Here's How To Navigate The Change With Resilience 187

LEADERSHIP TEAM

The Power Of Building A Leadership Team Manifesto...................195

How Team Coaching Can Help
Your Executive Team Lead As One 199

The Opportunity Your Executive Leadership Team
Could Be Missing 203

Don't Trust Your Team? Here's How To Start 207

SUCCESSION

Why You Need To Mentor Your Executive Leaders........................215

Why You Should Ditch Performance Reviews
(And What To Do Instead) 219

Passing The Torch: Your Guide To Succession Planning
And Development..223

How To Be An Effective Successor 227

Why A 360-Degree Assessment Isn't Enough
For Building Strong Leaders..231

Four Skillsets You Can Always Work On
To Improve As A Leader 235

CULTURE

How To Build A True Following As A Leader 243

How To Be A Champion For Women In Leadership.......................247

How To Encourage And Grow A Positive Culture
Throughout Your Organization 251

Hire Slow And Fire Fast: Why Leaders Should
Heed This Advice 255

Leadership Is A Customer Service Job—For Your Team
And Beyond 259

Successful Acquisitions Care About Culture 263

STRATEGY

Diversity Isn't An Outcome;
It's A Strategy For Business Success..271

How To Immediately Improve Your Strategic Plan...........................275

Why Reflection Is Crucial To Leadership,
Future Planning And Success 279

Your Short-Term Decisions Could Unintentionally
Create Long-Term Pain 283

Efficiency Is Just One Part Of An Effective Leader's Toolkit...........287

FOREWORD

Growing up in a rural community meant that we took our garbage to the dump ourselves. It was generally a monthly venture. And living at our local dump those days was a man named Monti. He lived in a trailer that someone had discarded. In fact, Monti's existence depended on what he found in other people's trash. My dad always made the effort to bring Monti a thermos of hot chocolate and would visit in his trailer whenever we unloaded our garbage. It was always painful for me to sit through their discussion. All I remember is that the trailer smelled bad. I never understood why dad took the time to talk to this man with a dirty beard and reeking worn out clothes. That is until the day my parents sold the farm and Monti road his old bike ten miles to come and say good-bye to my father. He had tears in his eyes the last time he and my father shook hands. I imagine dad was his only friend.

I understand today, after many years of working with and learning from a wide range of leaders, that those seeds of goodness planted in my formative years were my first exposure to leadership. I've learned from all my years in the leadership development field that, although ability matters in a leader, inner qualities matter more.

It is significant that recognizing the importance of these inner qualities has given rise to the concept of depth in leadership. When we talk of leadership now, the best leaders go beyond the rhetoric and address head-on issues of trust, character, integrity, and service. They tackle matters like self-awareness, core beliefs, and the meaning of life itself. However, attempting to simplify such issues in a world of speed and efficiency, the focus on depth is shackled by 100 word posts, sixty second YouTube videos, and superficial management fads. But humans can stand only so much triviality before we seek answers to such questions as, "What am I here for?" "How do I define success," and "What is the purpose of my life, of work, of being?" Indeed, it takes a conscious leader to sift through the chaff and excavate and execute on what truly matters.

It is the best leaders who have reached into the depths of themselves to wrestle with these questions and can thus help uncover, unleash, ferret out, extract, and inspire new ways of thinking and acting. This is essentially what true leadership is all about: helping humanity change the world by helping ourselves be more fully human.

In *The Inspired Leader*, Jenn does a masterful job of distilling and consolidating the core facets of leadership into a set of attributes and practical insights and tools that are accessible, understandable, and useful – without sacrificing depth. She cuts through superficial hype and gets to the core of what it takes to a be a great leader by being a good person, all the while keeping it simple. This is an art. And Jenn has mastered it.

In this marvelous work of art, you have at your fingertips timeless principles and tools to help you develop abilities as well as inner qualities through the challenges of daily leadership. You will find this to incredibly helpful reference book that covers what it means to embrace leadership, leadership styles, insights on emotional intelligence, the nature of boundaries and choices as a leader, increasing your capacity to foster accountability, succession, culture, and strategy, and attending to your own well-being as a leader. You can sit and be enriched in an afternoon read or use it as a reference guide to gain practical hands-on tools to respond to a specific leadership challenge you are facing.

This book is a product of years of work in the trenches as a leadership coach and consultant, as well as the CEO of successful company. Jenn has lived leadership and organizational culture for many years. She understands it from hands-on experience and truly embraces it – with wisdom, elegance, and simplicity. A skilled leadership advisor and good friend, Jenn and her team at Incito provide coaching and consulting for my team. I am confident referring clients because I know they will be professionally and competently taken care of.

For Jenn, leadership is distinct from positions of authority. The principles and tools encompassed in this book will support and guide anyone committed to amplifying their impact as a leader – with or without a title. In these pages, you will find inspiration and renewed perspectives on leadership and life through Jenn's insights. But it is in your own values, your own call to service, your own commitment to contribution, that you will ultimately find the sense of purpose that will compel you to work – and live – more consciously, authentically, and productively, with the greatest possible impact.

May we all take a step toward having our presence make this a better world. And may *The Inspired Leader* be a guide to you on your journey.

David Irvine
January, 2022

INTRODUCTION

Iwas always a top student in my class and I took great pride in that. But at 15, I suddenly found myself homeless and spent four months in a shelter. Not the way I had imagined what turning 16 would be like. Everything in my world was upside down. My sense of self, certainty and safety were gone. I went from being one of the top students in the entire school to a student who struggled just trying to GET to school. Let alone do well when I was there.

So when Mr. Rainsforth, my Automotive teacher, stopped me after class and asked to speak with me... I was sure I was in trouble. Instead he said *"You're the first student to pull out a book and voluntarily start reading in my class. Keep doing that."* I was stunned and completely unprepared to receive positive feedback. I stammered a response I can't remember, but I'll never forget that moment. While I was feeling like now one cared about me, he recognized and *acknowledged* my character at a time I couldn't even see it.

Mr. Rainsforth became a teacher I wanted to be proud of me and is the type of leader I still aspire to emulate decades later. He was a person who wanted to bring out the best in others. He believed in holding students to being their very best in character and in demonstrating the best results they were capable of. He was also a committed teacher and coach helping students learn skills that extended beyond the class into broader school achievement and life itself. I knew he was special at the time and today I recognize that Mr. Rainsforth was the first magnetic leader I had experienced.

This book was written to support you in becoming an even greater leader than you are today. The essays inside have been compiled over five years as my company has coached hundreds of leaders at all levels of organizations. From Manager to Director, from VP to CEO and everything in between.

The leaders came from almost every industry including Finance, Technology, Energy, Professional Services, Health, Manufacturing, Government, Non-Profit, Consumer Packaged Goods, Retail, Military, Emergency Services, Education, Transportation and so many more. It didn't take long to discover our clients struggled with the *same* challenges and opportunities, despite the diversity of their industries and roles.

It doesn't matter what industry you're in or what role you currently fill I promise you, whether you're struggling right now in your leadership or excelling and looking for new insights to become even more effective, this book has something for you as a leader.

Most of the leaders I've worked with have a lot on their minds and are seeking ideas to push their thinking on what is relevant right now in this moment. That's why the collection of short works you're about to read can each be read in five to ten minutes. I hope you read it from front to back eventually, but it's also been designed for micro-learning and inspiration.

Use this book like a leadership inspiration reference guide. Choose a topic that resonates with you and then jump to that section to find a quick perspective to shift your thinking. Come back again and find new inspiration to bring about new thinking for the next challenge or opportunity you face.

Thanks to Mr. Rainsforth's acknowledgment of my desire to read, today, my teenage daughter loves to read too. It only takes a few moments to see potential in people or opportunity in a system and add a little spark to encourage them forward. I hope this book inspires you to not only develop a new level of leadership in yourself; I hope it inspires you to develop the people, teams, culture and systems around you too.

EMBRACING LEADERSHIP

Dare to be different. Be a pioneer. Be a leader. Be the kind of [person] who, in the face of adversity, will continue to embrace life and walk fearlessly toward the challenge.

~ Oprah Winfrey

Accepting leadership can be daunting, exciting, bewildering, and fulfilling. It's a choice. I invite you to make the choice to embrace leadership. Doing so will mean that you must let go of thinking you have all the answers. You will also need to let go of winning at all costs or being liked by everyone all the time. Why? To reach your vision for the future by leading others to see it and join you in creating it.

What are you passionate about creating or contributing to? What is your vision for the future? Are you doing what others expect or relentlessly pursing indispensability in your current role to maintain the status quo? Or, are you getting clear on your vision and values and then making courageous choices to take baby steps forward yourself and with your team?

Authentic leadership looks like courage with solid boundaries and requires support because both stepping into the zone of courage and holding boundaries is incredibly hard. Leadership means embracing discomfort and understanding it doesn't get much more comfortable.

Discomfort is the zone of learning; effective leaders focus on continuous curiosity and learning and avoid shaming themselves for not knowing. As a result, great leaders understand that their personal development is critical to professional success. Embracing leadership means committing to being imperfect and continuing to grow and improve to best serve others and the vision for the future. This also means accepting that no one can lead on their own, even you. You must frequently talk to peers, a coach, and other people in your support network about your doubts, your difficult choices, for feedback, and to celebrate your wins.

Embracing leadership is a commitment to the unknown future.

LET GO OF WHAT YOU 'NEED TO KNOW'

As leaders climb the career ladder and take on greater responsibilities, they may begin to feel that they also need to know more about what is going on in the areas under their leadership. However, this can lead to information overload. You don't need to know everything, and you can delegate more than you think. Leaders, especially as they move into more senior positions, must strike a balance between knowing everything and being aware of just enough to do their job.

Start with establishing clear communication

Leaders need to find a balance between knowing how and what your team is doing and leaving them with enough autonomy so that they feel trusted with their work. We often fail to make clear commitments upfront with others, including our team members. Be sure to explain your expectations in detail. What is the outcome, goal or finished work? Are there specific quality expectations? Are they free to complete the work how they see fit as long as they meet the outcome expectations or do you need to outline how the work should be completed? Make sure to give the "why" of the project because it provides necessary context for the work.

For projects with longer timelines, I recommend creating milestone check-ins. This means your team member checks in with you, instead of you going to check in on them. Check-ins could be phased by time (i.e., weekly) or by task completion (i.e., once they've reached a certain stage of the work). What are your expectations for communication when things change? What can they expect from you when things change?

In today's workplace, your team may extend beyond the walls of your office. When working with remote teams, use video calls as much as you can and reserve phone calls for exceptional circumstances only. It's even more important to be clear about your expectations and ask your team members to recap for you. This will give you the opportunity to understand their concerns, questions and expectations and ensure that you're both on the same page about the work that needs to be done.

What you actually need to know changes as your responsibility increases

Some leaders who are early in their careers, or are used to working with smaller teams, might be accustomed to having clear communication with direct reports. However, as you move up within an organization, your direct reports may have their own direct reports. Does this mean that you have to know what your direct reports are doing as well as what their direct reports are doing?

The ideal level of direct communication with your immediate reports varies depending on the scope of work and seniority of the individuals that work for you. If you lead frontline workers, you may have more of a supervisory role. If you manage a self-directed team of experienced technical professionals or knowledge workers, you may require less frequent communication. I recommend a weekly or biweekly one-to-one meeting for open dialogue along with any necessary reporting back.

It is important to hold your direct reports accountable. Ask them questions about what level or type of support they might need to meet expectations. Know and respect your roles and boundaries, and make sure not to overreach. I have great concern for leaders who go around their direct reports. If this is someone you try to get around on a regular basis, are they even a fit for your team in the first place? Are they competent in their role? If not, how can you coach them to be competent? If the question is around their integrity, you will have to deal with those consequences if you don't give them the support they need to perform.

Address concerns around reporting details

Who needs to know what, and what level of detail do they need to know? This is a question that helps define what you need to know as a leader and as someone who reports to upper management. When reporting to your own boss, you can provide high-level information. If they ask for further detail, it's okay to push back and ask what their concerns are. You can say, "I don't have that answer for you at the moment. Let me get back to you on that."

When it comes to the details that you actually need, I recommend reminding yourself of what I call the 80/20 ratio. In short, 80% of what you ask is what you want to know, and only 20% is what you actually need to know: context of current work, overall trends, outcomes and analysis of work and the evolving impact of what your team is doing. Oftentimes leaders ask for more details when they come from expert-type roles where they used to do the work, and they want to compare that with how it's being done now. Cross-functional leaders who are now managing teams where they do not have expertise are more likely to trust the teams and the experts within.

Learn when to let go

Let go of perfectionism in order to understand what you actually need to know in your role. You cannot know everything. You don't have an answer for every question, but you can get answers for questions that come up. As a leader your role will likely involve more long-term strategy work and fewer day-to-day tasks. If you are overloading yourself with the minutiae, you cannot perform in your own job, especially when you begin to lead other leaders.

Learn the drivers of your need to know everything. What are you trying to prevent? What are you trying to achieve? How else might you work toward that outcome in partnership with your team or direct reports? What are the most essential details you must know to report to your senior leadership and/or to complete your work? As you answer these questions, you'll define what you truly "need" to know.

QUESTIONING YOUR LEADERSHIP ABILITY? HERE'S HOW TO CAST AWAY THE DOUBT

"*What am I doing?*"

*W*If you're a leader and this question is plaguing you, trust me, you're not alone. With 70% of people having felt like an imposter at least one time in their lives, regardless of gender or occupation, this very question is afflicting those around you as well. Time and again, I work with successful leaders who are questioning their own leadership.

Whether you are feeling overwhelmed by responsibilities, going through changes in the nature of your role or even if you've been promoted through your organization over time, second-guessing your leadership skills is normal.

So, how do you move through these feelings of uncertainty?

First things first: Figure out what you're actually questioning. Are you not sure if you're cut out for leadership, or is it that you're uncertain if you want your specific leadership role?

Am I cut out for this?

You may be putting your successes down to "luck," feeling like your time is never your own, or are constantly reacting to situations, fearful that someone may find out that you don't know what you're doing.

It takes courage to admit that you don't know it all, but this admission goes a long way to start removing these doubts about your skills. What can you do?

1. Don't pretend that you have nothing to learn.

There's a shift when you start showing that you're open to learning and start being more engaged with the work you have in front of you. By removing the pressure of "I have to know it all," you create space in your mind to remain curious and keep learning.

2. Be willing to risk personal exposure.

Let your team know what you're working on. When you're vulnerable with your team about where you're at, you show them you're human. This creates more of a connection with them, as you're quietly giving them permission to not be perfect either and supporting them through their own journey of discovery.

3. Look for possibilities in not knowing.

Stop with the "I should be able to" mindset because even if you "should," you don't. But by being willing to learn, you find possibilities. Try something different, understanding that new processes and strategies might not work, and that's OK. Change your mindset from "people will think less of me" to "I might look weak, but I get excited about the work I'm now doing because I'm having fun again."

Start listening to your own self-talk when these thoughts trickle into your mind. Identify what you're feeling in order to move forward. As you learn new tactics and discover new skill sets, chances are you'll find that you are cut out for the leadership role (if it's something you want) because you're showing what a leader is: someone who remains curious, looks for ways to be more strategic, empowers their team by demonstrating vulnerability, and is always willing to grow.

Do I even want this?

This is a fair question, but I challenge you to ask yourself this: If you were to choose this leadership role today, why would you choose it? This will help you move from a place of feeling stuck in your role to a place of *choosing* your role. When you doubt whether you want a role, it's often when you didn't choose it, but were promoted into it.

Questions to help you in this mindset include:

- Is this an issue with being a leader, or is it leading at the particular organization you're in?

- Is this an issue with your specific leadership role, or is it that you really don't want to be a leader?

The key here is to find your answers without judgment. You may not want to actually be a leader, and that's OK. But if you discover that you would choose this leadership, then it's important to get clear on the value you provide from a leadership perspective by looking at your accomplishments to date. And remember that "leader" successes are often longer term rather than immediate.

Find support

Leadership is one of the hardest things to do, so it's important to understand that questioning your leadership is not rare or wrong. However, the bravery to move through these uncertain feelings doesn't have to be done through big, sweeping acts. Your bravery can be as simple as starting to talk. Give yourself permission to tell someone who has earned your trust how you're feeling.

It's also important that leaders build a diverse support team around them. This can look like:

- Leaders who are leading alongside you

- Mentors who can share their own stories and wisdom

- A coach who brings an objective mirror to reflect your story back to you

- Friends, even if they don't fully understand what you do, who are your empathetic confidants

Without a support team, your thoughts will grow, perhaps resulting in anxiety, depression, or self-sabotage, which erodes your leadership over time. You can lose track of what you love not just in your work, but in other areas of your life that used to fulfill you.

The last thing I want is for you to stew in your questioning. No matter how long you've been in your role, if you are doubting where you are, start talking. A simple admission to someone you trust can open a world of possibilities for growth and finding more fulfillment in life.

FOR SENIOR EXECUTIVES, PERSONAL DEVELOPMENT IS PROFESSIONAL DEVELOPMENT

As leaders work their way up the corporate ladder, it's likely that they have taken advantage of professional development opportunities along the way. They may have taken courses, attended conferences and upskilled where they could. But what happens once you get to the top? How can executives continue to grow as leaders?

Why Executive Leaders Need To Keep Growing

As you progress into executive leadership, professional development might look different. Just because you have reached the perceived pinnacle of your career does not mean that you have reached the pinnacle of your effectiveness and impact.

Executives have the difficult job of thinking about the world from different perspectives, including those of their employees, stakeholders, customers and everyone in between. One day you might have to speak with a business partner experiencing challenges. Another day you might have to work with a department that has just gone through budget cuts. As an executive, you need to be attuned to all of that at any given time, having to navigate through situations where there is no set outcome.

Executives must be able to maintain composure and stability amid tough situations and practice compassion and empathy. They need to develop a systems-thinking view and make connections between ideas or decisions and have an understanding of the interconnectedness of those within the organization, within the industry and beyond. They also need to be able to balance compassion with boundaries.

Shifting Professional Development Needs

In the early years of your career, professional development opportunities are plentiful. It is easier to identify any skills gaps that you may need to fill, whether you want to specialize in your role and pursue further education or you want to master a wider range of skills and therefore seek complementary opportunities. Not only are you able to identify the skills that you would like to develop, you are also able to find a variety of professional development opportunities to fulfill your needs.

However, once you move into senior leadership, professional development is not as straightforward. Demands and responsibilities change as you move up within an organization. These roles typically require less specific skills and technical knowledge. Executives need to be proficient in people leadership, business management, strategy, systems thinking, vision, inspiration and innovation. Therefore, professional development for leaders now calls for opportunities to develop not skill, but mindset.

Where C-Suite Leaders Can Find Professional Development Opportunities

For CEOs, personal development is professional development. Exposure to different perspectives helps shore up the leadership mindset, moving away from functional expertise and into strategic thinking. However, there are no specific courses or workshops for that. CEOs might plan for leadership retreats for their teams or boards but not really seek opportunities for themselves. Here are some examples of experiences in which senior executives can develop the leadership mindset.

- **Board roles in non-profits.** The boards of nonprofit organizations are often composed of professionals from varying backgrounds working for the same cause. Joining such a board gives you exposure to different ways of thinking, ideas and situations that you may not normally run into.

- **Mentorship (peers, same industry and diverse industries).** The benefits of mentorship are well known, but at this level, senior executives may have outgrown their internal mentors. They could seek peer mentorship, even in the same industry with someone who might be further along in their role. The most overlooked opportunity is mentorship from individuals outside of their industry. The perspective of someone in a similar role but in a different industry is essential for innovation, vision and strategic thinking.

- **CEO roundtables.** Much like peer mentorship, CEO roundtables provide a safe space for senior executives to share their experiences with others and, depending on the forum, could offer perspectives from a wide range of organizations.

- **Executive coaching.** While mentors can provide valuable insights, they may not always be objective since they are bringing their own experiences into the partnership. An executive coach can be a valuable resource for leaders. They come from a place with less bias and can challenge you in a different way because they are not attached to what you want to do next like someone connected to your business may be.

- **Personal board of advisors.** Just as a board advises a CEO, you can build your own personal board of advisors for "Me, Inc." This is a group of people from different backgrounds who can advise you on different areas of your life because they are supporting one thing: you.

- **360° assessment.** I always start my clients with a 360° assessment because there is so much to learn from the results. These assessments ask for both your personal view of your leadership as well as that of your team and where they do or do not line up. It provides the leader with a starting point to create an action plan based on what they learned from the assessment: a perfect growth opportunity.

- **Reading about strategy, leadership and managing people (emotional intelligence).** In this case, valuable reading materials for CEOs are ones that are about expanding your perspective, not teaching specific skills. Business-focused books can expose you to other ways of thinking and develop your judgment, risk-taking, direction and strategy.

- **Leading a different business function outside of your functional expertise.** Although you might have some understanding of the different roles or departments within your organization, there is no better way to learn than to work within those functions and enrich your knowledge of their perspectives.

Always Make Time For Growth

Some leaders think about development for everyone else but not themselves, not out of complacence or arrogance, but perhaps because they have forgotten about themselves or don't know where to begin. You never know it all or have it all figured out. This world of volatility, uncertainty, complexity and ambiguity (VUCA) is ever-changing, and you must evolve with society, your industry and your organization to lead your teams into the future.

IT'S LONELY AT THE TOP: DEALING WITH IMPOSTER SYNDROME AT THE EXECUTIVE LEVEL

Imposter syndrome has become a popular topic over the years, and rightly so. Many of us have had feelings of inadequacy, of being unworthy or undeserving of where we're at in life or at work, and have even thought that one day we might be exposed as a fraud.

Research has shown that up to 70% of people will experience imposter syndrome at least once in their lives. The good news is that we are recognizing the signs of imposter syndrome and more people are talking about it.

However, I've found that those conversations are more common among new leaders. As professionals climb the corporate ladder, conversations about imposter syndrome become fewer and farther in between, and that's not good.

What Imposter Syndrome Can Look And Feel Like

We all deal with inner voices that tell us good and bad things. You can spot imposter syndrome by noticing thoughts and feelings that include:

- Feelings of self-doubt, whether in your ability to be effective in your role as a whole, or in decisions you make and your ability to make them

- Feelings of unworthiness of our accomplishments or attention from others; feelings of being unworthy in your role at work

- Feelings of fraudulence or being a phony; feeling that you're just a minute from being found out, or that you don't know what you're doing and/or don't know enough

- Thinking your skills are nothing special no matter how skilled you are in your field or specialty

- Attributing your successes to luck or to others; being overly modest and not owning your accomplishments and talents (i.e., "I didn't do anything—my team did it all and I just got out of the way.")

- Sidestepping accomplishments and recognition out of discomfort

These negative thoughts are fear-based. Biologically, your body responds to fear in a protective manner. This is why I sometimes refer to these voices as your "inner security guard." Ignoring the feelings will not make them go away, so we have to learn to live with them and address them in a healthy manner.

Why Imposter Syndrome Becomes More Difficult For Executives

The best antidote for imposter syndrome is to talk to others about your thoughts and the feelings you're experiencing, but I've found the circle of trust often becomes smaller for leaders and executives. They have fewer mentors and people who feel like they can talk to honestly. They feel more pressure to be perfect and to deliver.

A senior leader may have an amplified experience of imposter syndrome because they feel like they have more people relying on them. Even though they most likely have enjoyed a successful career leading up to their promotion, they may also feel like they have not earned their position, like they were only lucky to have been chosen for it.

Executive positions often equate to high-stress roles that can quickly wear you out. If you have perfectionist tendencies, you may suffer over every small mistake while pushing yourself without feeling fulfillment in your role.

How To Deal With Imposter Syndrome, Especially As An Executive

You can't prevent the feelings of imposter syndrome, but you can raise your awareness and take action to work through them. Those inner voices—that I refer to as the "committee of idiots"—will come up, but if they are spotted early, they can be addressed and reframed so you can practice resilience.

Remember that you are not the only person who feels this way. There is nothing like talking to someone else about your feelings of self-doubt, and the best way to get comfortable with asking for help is to start, even if that means starting slow at first. Talk to peers, mentors and coaches. Ask your mentors and peers about times they've felt in over their heads and experienced similar feelings of self-doubt.

Although it might seem like you have fewer peers in your position, you can always reach out to others who might have previously been in a similar situation. For example, I've worked with a mayor whose town was devastated by a flood. He went through great challenges, short term and long term, that seemed one of a kind. Years later, another mayor whose town was ravaged by a wildfire reached out to him to talk. Even though they had never met before, they connected with one another through their shared experiences.

If you feel like you can't talk to just anybody, allow yourself to be vulnerable with those who have earned the right. They could be long-term mentors, or even peers in similar roles but completely different industries. Coaches and mental health professionals can also be part of this circle. It is important to cultivate a wider support network around you with whom you can freely express your feelings.

Mentoring others also helps to reconnect with the wisdom you possess and recognize your strengths and expertise. Sometimes we forget how much we know and all that we have experienced. This reaffirms that you have something that not everybody has. People look up to you for a reason.

Most importantly, practice self-compassion. Be kind to yourself. Challenge your expectations of yourself, especially where they might be unrealistic.

We Need To Keep Talking About Imposter Syndrome

We tend to believe we are the only ones who feel this way. Left unchecked, these feelings can lead you to derail your own career. It can hold you back from sharing your ideas and from accepting promotions or challenging projects for which you are qualified.

With increased light on imposter syndrome, we can feel freer to be honest about our feelings and reinforce to ourselves that we do belong. It's important for us to have feelings of worthiness of our talents. If we want to be healthy leaders, we need to understand where imposter syndrome shows up and work through those feelings.

IS YOUR HUMILITY HURTING YOU? WHAT HAPPENS WHEN YOU ACKNOWLEDGE YOUR VALUE

As leaders, we're told to be humble when it comes to accepting credit for our teams' wins. But, when we deflect the credit we're given, we actually minimize our own efforts and impact. It's an interesting paradox to be in.

So, how can we confidently accept credit without feeling like imposters, as though we're bragging or taking credit away from our team?

To Accept Or Not To Accept?

We all have different reasons for accepting credit (or not). The first thing to acknowledge is why you want to start accepting your credit in the first place. When I ask clients about why they don't want to own their credit, we always discover what accepting credit will actually do for them and their team. Reasons that come through as to the benefits of accepting credit are vast, including:

- **You need to hear it.** Just as you're a cheerleader for your team, helping them acknowledge their own successes and strengths, you need this as well. Notice how your team members perform once they've heard and accepted a compliment. Are they more confident, committed or driven? It works the same for you.

- **You add more value.** By acknowledging the skills you bring and value you create, you allow yourself to apply more of these skills, adding even more value as a leader.

- **Build credibility.** When you deflect credit given, people question your leadership — whether consciously or not — as your deflection casts doubts on your ability to lead. When you acknowledge the contribution(s) you add, you build others' confidence in your leadership, your team and your organization.

- **Build authority.** By owning your contributions, you understand your direct impact. You're able to demonstrate what you can achieve, drawing people to you. Think of Elon Musk: a great example of someone who can talk about what he's done and someone people want to follow in droves. He doesn't talk about his successes in a bragging way but in a factual way that inspires.

- **Create stronger relationships.** Accepting credit given to you helps create stronger relationships. When you don't accept credit from someone, you're basically saying "I don't believe you" or "You don't know what you're talking about." By accepting, you demonstrate trust in their opinion.

What's important to remember is that just because you start to give yourself credit doesn't mean that you're taking credit from your team. Rather, you're acknowledging the role you played in supporting your team's success. Own this without downplaying your contributions.

Owning Your Credit

It's okay to feel uncomfortable when accepting credit. To move through these feelings, start

- **Noticing your self-talk.** Do you think that you didn't have much to do with a success? Notice what crops up for you during these times and start to change your inner dialogue to one of "I deserve credit because of [x]." Highlight in your mind the role you played, and acknowledge your part in your team's success.

- **Recognizing when you deflect.** Your successes are not due to luck. You may have been at the right place at the right time for the success to happen, but you still took action. Luck only takes success so far. You led your team along the path to success, so why are you deflecting?

- **Thinking of your resume.** Consider what you've achieved as a leader and how your leadership helped your team succeed; this is what you should be proud to put on your resume. Downplaying your abilities doesn't do anyone any favors.

- **Telling people.** Whether you share your accomplishments or your learnings, just start telling people. Trust that people want to know what you're doing. Plus, a happy side effect to sharing is that this helps you get clear on where you want to go next.

- **Working with imposter feelings.** Acknowledge that maybe someone could have done something better or different than you did — but they didn't. You did it. You're the one who did what needed to be done. Even if this is you not believing in your skills as a leader, you were given the role as leader and you accepted. The role would not have been offered to you if you didn't have leadership skills.

- **Getting specific.** If a simple "thank you" doesn't sit well with you, then be specific about the parts both you and your team played in a success. If you asked questions of your team, talk about how this encouraged your people to get curious and find a solution. This is just as important as finding the solution itself.

- **Giving positive feedback to others.** Notice when they deflect credit given. Hold them in their own discomfort and encourage them to say thank you. Focus on helping others on their journey and you'll see in them what you need to work on in yourself.

To begin accepting credit, you must first choose to own your part in your team's success. You're not going to start accepting credit and growing your confidence in yourself unless you make the choice to do so. The crux is about choosing to own your wins; the rest is just tactics.

Imagine what impact you can have when you start to accept your earned credit.

STOP DOING WHAT YOU 'SHOULD' DO AND TURN YOUR THOUGHTS INTO ACTION

Choosing to do nothing is an excuse to stay stuck. Harsh, perhaps, but true. Listen, I get it: We're coming into the last quarter of the year and are starting to think about what we have to do before the year ends. We're noting that what we *want* to accomplish may not connect with our "have to" list. When we start thinking about this, we sometimes find ourselves in the "I don't even know what I want, so I'm not going to do anything" mindset, leading to inaction.

When I hear from clients, "I don't know what I want," there's often a bigger problem than what's being acknowledged. So, whether you're trying to figure out if you want to get a promotion, step into a leadership role or complete a half marathon before the year's out, the first step is acknowledging that doing nothing is not OK.

Should Vs. Must Debate

As explained in Elle Luna's book, *The Crossroads of Should and Must*, we face the indecision of what we believe we *should* do over what we know we *must* do.

- **Should:** These are the expectations and obligations that others put on us, whether it's our culture, society, community, business, family or friends. Decisions we make on this basis feel heavy and are often made for someone or something else.

- **Must:** Our "must" is what we feel drawn to: our convictions, dreams, longings and knowing. When we make decisions from this place, we may not necessarily be happy, but we feel fulfilled because we know we made a decision for ourselves and not for others.

What I've witnessed—and experienced—is indecision often arises when our "shoulds" are in conflict with our "musts." Think of it this way: You should be looking to move up the corporate ladder, but do you really want to?

Coming from a place of must, you're better able to determine what you want to take action on in a way that will fulfill you. So, where do you start?

1. **Increase your self-awareness.** Until you're aware of your "shoulds" and "musts," it's hard to find your path forward. Write down what *you* might want. When you visualize these things, you connect with them. If they stay in your head, they become bigger and more overwhelming. Yes, you may feel silly writing these goals down, but no one has to know what you're doing, so there's no judgment. For instance, if you're thinking about stepping into a CEO role, write it down. Then write down your other options, like taking an early retirement, taking a sabbatical before entering that CEO role, or even staying in your current role. Write down all the things you might want, without limitations.

2. **Write down what you *don't* want.** Not sure what you want? That's OK! Sometimes, to get clear on what we want, we have to first become clear about what we don't.

3. **Pay attention to your feelings.** By getting our wants down on paper, we begin to discover some of our options. Note that options are

not decisions. What I've seen is that we'll often go after the more rational choice, but this may be in conflict with our must. You may even discover conflicting emotions. Know that it's perfectly OK to be afraid and excited at the same time. Simply take note of how you're feeling.

4. **Start talking to people about your options.** Ask questions and collect information from those who've done something similar to your goal. For example, if you're thinking of transitioning to a CEO role, talk to other CEOs and ask them about what assumptions they had that were true and not true, what regrets they have, what they're grateful for, and if they would take the same path again.

Beware of analysis paralysis, as waiting for the "right" choice to appear will never happen. Once you've collected information, pick a goal on your list for now. You'll learn about yourself just by picking something to move towards, and it will get you out of being stuck.

When you make decisions from a place of must, what's important to you will come forward. With this choice, you know where you're going—at least for now.

There Are No Wrong Choices, Only Next Choices

When you've picked a goal, give yourself permission to change it if it's not working. You can always evolve your goal along the way by asking why it isn't working and what you have learned from it. Your goal doesn't always have to be bigger and better. The change will help bring clarity to what you truly want—what your musts are.

If you're not currently fulfilled, no longer is "I don't know what I want" a credible excuse to stay where you are. The only way to move forward is by making a choice, then tweaking along the way.

If you're waiting for that magical spark of suddenly knowing, it simply won't happen. You have to work for it. Take control of your choices to finish the year by understanding what you should do and must do, and start turning your thoughts into real action.

LEADERSHIP STYLE

Debate is common about which leadership style is most effective.
The answer, of course … it all depends.

~ Thomas Kohntopp

Every leader is unique and has a particular style and reputation. The style most effective for you is discovered through self-awareness, by embracing your uniqueness, and developing the mindset of leadership. On top of it all, you must adapt your leadership style to the people and circumstances you encounter.

While we may idealize having the "whole leadership package" the reality is that having a unique style makes you more effective. We all want to be relatable and achieving leaders, strategic and influencing leaders, passionate and steady leaders. But, to embrace every style equally would leave others confused about who you really are and how to follow you.

The path to your unique style requires a personal development journey of releasing the need to be an expert and developing a mindset of creating for the future. It requires you to be courageous in letting go of pleasing, protecting, and controlling, and instead, shifting to recognizing the choices you have even when it feels like you have no choice.

Your choices are guided by the values shaped by who you are and your life experiences.

Knowing and developing your leadership style is an important part of self-awareness. It is the cornerstone of intentional leadership.

WHY YOU CAN'T BE BOTH A LEADER AND AN EXPERT

Leadership – this is where your success as an expert has taken you. But while you thrived as an expert, you now find your expertise is actually hindering you in your leadership role.

Why is that?

As an expert, you had the answers, or at least the resources and techniques to find them. As a leader, your role is now to support your team in finding the answers themselves. This mindset transition is often overlooked, resulting in a lack of clarity about your role, sometimes for years. What, then, are your typical responsibilities as a leader? Leaders:

- Strategically think and develop future solutions

- Empower their teams and maximize their potential

- Let their teams fail

- Are proactive, not reactive

- Provide critical and curious feedback to their teams

- Become experts at asking questions, not giving answers

A leader is meant to bring their team to another level. An expert is part of the solution that the leader is creating.

Expert Mindset Hindering Your Leadership?

When my executive-level clients straddle this line between their old identity as "expert" and their new one as "leader," it's clear that when they refuse to let go of their expert mindset, they experience:

- Burnout: They feel that they have to do everything all the time and have all the answers.

- Conflicts with team members: They always give their expertise, often with closed ears.

- Inadequacy: They're uncertain how to be successful as a leader. The Peter principle tells us this happens because people are promoted due to their past successes, but can only succeed so far as their inadequacies allow them to. Without understanding their gaps in mindset and training, a leader will ultimately fail.

Moving From Expert To Leader

Don't worry– it's not all doom and gloom for leaders. Below are a few proactive steps you can take to ease your transition from an expert to a leader mindset.

1. Frame your role.

Get clear on what your role actually is. Write your own job description outlining what you're supposed to be doing now. For example:

- Grow and develop your team.

- Use critical thinking to identify future opportunities and challenges.

- Build relationships across your organization for the betterment and support of your team.

- Help your team remove roadblocks, without doing it for them.

- Ask questions and identify gaps in the ideas your team provides.

Getting clear on your role today makes your team more effective for tomorrow. Ultimately, your role is not about problem-solving – that's your team's job. Your role is coaching, mentoring, developing, strategic thinking, supporting your team (not vice versa) and creating for the future.

2. Become more self-aware.

Begin noting when you want to jump in and be the "expert" with your team. This means understanding when you want to provide a solution rather than ask a question. If you're not sure where to begin, ask your team and peers where they see you jumping in as an expert.

A great question my clients use is, "Where do you see me voicing my opinion rather than asking questions?" Note the consistencies in their answers and make a conscious effort to pay attention to these times.

3. Develop leader technique strategies.

I've said it before and I'll say it again: Leaders are not born. They are developed and supported in this role. Strategies for building a successful leader mindset include:

- Training with a coach to understand how to effectively support and develop your team

- Creating reminders for yourself and reviewing them before you sit down with your team

- Recognizing that it's okay for your team to fail in certain instances, then exploring what they've learned during your debrief of the "failure"

- Developing a list of go-to questions to keep yourself in a curious place and to gain a better understanding of your team's point of view. For example: "Can you walk me through your thinking?" "How did you come to this decision?" "What led you to choose X over Y?"

I often liken the expert/leader mindset transition to that of writer/editor. A writer brings their expertise in creative thinking, grammar, spelling, etc. An editor brings curiosity to the writer's work, looking for flow issues, gaps in content, missing information, why things are written a certain way and so forth. The editor elevates the writer's work not by saying "this is how it should be written," but by asking questions. Raise your team's work by asking questions.

Setting Yourself Up For Leadership Success

The mistake we often make is promoting people because of their expertise, without considering that we're actually putting them through a career change. It's incorrect to assume that just because someone succeeds in their role as an expert (often a reactionary role), that they'll also succeed as a leader (a proactive role).

Developing a successful leader mindset is really a lesson of letting go, becoming vulnerable, and transitioning from solution finder to curious questioner. If you are a leader and seeking ideas for what may be holding you back, start by exploring whether your expertise is actually the culprit. Become the leader you want to be, and let your team be the experts.

WHAT TYPE OF LEADER
DO YOU WANT TO BE?

Leadership styles are not one-size-fits-all. In fact, there are a number of different types of leaders, all with different strengths and weaknesses. While there are many leadership styles, the real question isn't about what type of leader you are, but about what type of leader you want to be. Knowing this, you can redirect your strengths to become the leader you want.

In working with my clients, we've explored different leadership skill sets to highlight reactive versus strategic leadership, along with the strengths and effectiveness of each style. Once clients identify where they are now, we then build strategies to move them toward who they want to be.

Reactive Leadership

A common concern I hear from new clients is that they are always reacting to fires, never moving forward or completing strategic work. This is because they are typically leading from a reactive mindset, often falling into one of the following three types:

1. **Controllers:** *If I'm not perfect, I'm not good enough.*

Controllers rely on perfection, often leading to overwhelming and extreme control to make sure they and their team are perfect. A controller believes

- in control, not delegation.

- anything less than perfect is not okay.

- winning is a must; failure is not an option.

- in setting unachievable, unrealistically high standards, resulting in a burnt-out team.

While controllers can damage their relationships, they do have a number of strengths, including an ability to achieve short-term results, the willingness to take risks with decisions, and confidence to voice opinions, even if they're controversial.

To become more effective, controllers must let go of their fear of failure.

2. Protectors: *If I'm not right, I'm not good enough.*

Protectors tend to be distant, focused on protecting their organization. Often, they will have the underlying belief that to be right, they have to point out flaws in others. Other traits include

- asking critical, not constructive, questions.

- coming across as uncaring or insensitive.

- being unreceptive to feedback.

- not moving forward without knowing what's "right."

That said, protectors have gifts, such as the ability to objectively analyze a situation, deeply caring for their organization, and carrying great wisdom because they observe and explore before acting.

For protectors, a big hurdle is moving their leading approach from overly critical thinking and questioning to providing constructive feedback, helping others find their own answers.

3. Pleasers: *If I'm not liked, I'm not good enough.*

Pleasers do not want to rock the boat, but keep the peace. With this need to be liked, they

- always look for feedback before acting.

- aren't assertive, but tend to be passively aggressive.

- do not make decisions, often abdicating – not delegating – this responsibility to others.

- struggle to be seen as a leader.

While pleasers do have their faults, their positive traits often include being very reliable, creating harmony between people, and having good listening skills.

For pleasers, it's important to find ways to be more direct in their communication style and let go of being liked by everyone, helping to create a more efficient team.

Strategic Leadership

On the flip side, rather than being reactive, a leader can be strategic. There are two types of strategic leadership styles that I've seen as being effective in building productive, happy teams: relators and achievers.

Relators focus on growth and sustainability for their individual team members. They tend to be charismatic, focused on development and coaching, and committed to having strong relationships. Relators are willing to use themselves as examples, showing their team how to be vulnerable to grow their skill sets and reach specific goals.

Similar to relators in skill sets, achievers focus on growth and sustainability for the betterment of their organization. While they focus on individual growth for team members, this is typically to support the bigger picture achievement and outcome they want.

Becoming The Leader You Want To Be

If you've identified with a reactive leader type, that's great, as being aware of your strengths and weaknesses is important. To move forward, it becomes about mindset shifts to create small, incremental changes to use your strengths proactively. Steps can include:

- **Work on vulnerability**

  Moving from a reactive leader into a strategic one takes vulnerability. After all, you're opening yourself up to criticism, all while stepping outside of your comfort zone. This work helps you focus on using your strengths in a more strategic and proactive way.

- **Stop being the expert**

  Leaders are just that— leaders. However, you likely moved into a leader role because of the expertise you showed previously. Here, you need to reframe your mindset, becoming the curious leader, rather than the subject matter expert.

- **Use your strengths**

  As highlighted above, each leader type—whether reactive or strategic—has its strengths. The trick is learning how to use your strengths to move into a place of effective leadership. Focus on enhancing your style from your strengths, not your fears.

We all have a tendency to believe that we're in a positive space and avoid admitting that we might be reactive leaders. But acceptance and acknowledgment of both your strengths and inefficiencies are the first steps to becoming a great leader. How are you holding yourself back from being effective? There's no shame, only knowledge and growth based on your strengths that allow you to grow into the leader you want to be.

THE APPROACHABLE LEADER: ADAPTING YOUR STYLE TO WORK FOR YOUR EMPLOYEES

The higher you move up in your career, the more direct and indirect reports you are likely to have. But as you grow, how can you develop a style of leadership that works for everyone?

Leadership And Management Go Hand In Hand

There are two sides to your role when you have direct reports: leadership and management. Some may even use the two terms interchangeably, and the two concepts do overlap.

Leadership is about developing potential, whether it be in people, projects or processes. It's also about setting a direction and helping others see the vision. It's strategic thinking and finding ways to improve. It's helping people develop, whether it's in their individual career paths, or helping them see their work in the context of the company vision.

Management, on the other hand, is about getting tasks done and managing the business day to day. It's the daily firefighting, delegating tasks and asking for accountability from your employees. Management ensures execution to create short-term results; leadership creates long-term impact. In business, we need both. Bringing the two practices together gets us where we need to be.

There may be pressure on senior leaders and executives to lead and not manage because we make it seem like leading is better. But in reality, leading and managing is a spectrum that you need to be able to move through. If you are too focused on the long-term vision, you may miss out on managing the day-to-day execution that follows through on that vision. Focusing solely on the day-to-day is like running a race looking down at your feet so you don't trip, but losing the race to another runner who was focused on the finish line.

Leadership And Management Styles: Not One-Size-Fits-All

What is the best way to lead and manage everyone? The answer to that starts first and foremost with finding a leadership style that works for you. Understand your personality preferences and leadership development strengths. From there, you can adjust your style to meet the individual needs of your employees.

Becoming a leader of people also requires a mindset shift: You need to see your team members as people first and employees second. This may seem overly simplistic, but knowing the context of their experiences and their lives helps you understand what they need and how you can work together in a way that will help you meet in the middle. Maybe one employee is an active community volunteer with years of board experience. Another might have had a previous career in another industry. Partner with each person to understand what they need to be most effective and successful.

Hold each employee as creative, resourceful and whole. This is a concept that we use in leadership coaching but also applies to employee coaching. This means that they are accountable for themselves, their learning and their outcomes as well as the help and support they require to achieve their goals. Let them fail, but show them that you are there to support them if they need it.

You cannot be a chameleon and change your management style completely for each person. Rather, you begin with a framework and adapt it to meet the unique developmental needs of each team member. For example, a leader I coach is starting to have one-to-one development conversations with her team members, and although she has a general framework that applies to everyone, the frequency for early-career employees is different than seasoned employees. The weight and context of each conversation will vary according to the needs and development of each team member. Additionally, this leader takes a direct approach with some of her staff while deploying a softer approach for others.

We all need three things to succeed and be happy: autonomy, meaningful relationships and meaningful work. This is a three-legged stool, but each employee will need a different mix to feel satisfied at work.

How To Show Approachability

There are things you can do to show your employees that you are approachable. Whenever you have the opportunity, tell stories of how you have handled challenging situations in the past. Show employees how you come to your decisions, not just what decisions you made. This helps them understand you and how you think. They may not always agree with the decisions you make, but at least they know what to expect from you. An approachable leader is one who is reliable and consistent.

You must also stay open and listen. Embrace compassion and step into empathy. Approachable leaders ask lots of questions before giving out answers or making any conclusions and jumping to assumptions about what their team members need. Sometimes it's hard not to get paternalistic or maternalistic, especially when dealing with an employee with less career experience. Leaders often feel that they need to step in and rescue the employee or the task at hand. When employees tell them about a problem, effective leaders provide support through it rather than take it over. They have more hard conversations, not fewer. They approach conversations from a place where they show that the other person is not broken, not someone whose gaps they need to fill. The team member will feel that they can ask for the support they need from their leader.

Ultimately, you must find a balance: You manage the task, and you lead the person. Know your strengths because they will be your go-to easy place. Find ways to lean on them in a leadership capacity. You can be a task-focused leader who can build good relationships to get tasks done. Or you can be a relationship-focused leader that still sees projects over the finish line and achieves results. Being aware of where you are starting will help you adapt your own style to the needs of your employees.

BECOMING A MAGNETIC LEADER: HOW TO DRAW THE POTENTIAL FROM YOUR PEOPLE

"Leaders don't convince people to follow them. Leaders walk forward, and those who want to go down their path decide to follow." – Simon Sinek

Have you ever been in the presence of a leader who draws you in, engages you, and helps pull your talents and skills out, inspiring you to continue growing? Someone who seems magnetic, pulling people forward with them, rather than pushing them? This is a pull leader, one who attracts people to them, inspiring growth, dedication and results.

So, what exactly is the difference between a pull leader and a push one? If pull is so effective, why aren't all leaders using this style of leadership?

Push Leadership

Push leaders typically spend a lot of time convincing their team that a direction is the right one, trying to sell ideas, rather than having people buy into them. This often results in either (1) unnecessary hustle by the leader (chasing, following up, micro-managing, etc.) or (2) a dictatorship-style of leadership where the leader falls into the "do it because I said so" mindset.

Push leaders are often great at achieving short-term results, with lots of small wins along the way. However, this type of leadership doesn't engage a team and won't see long-term sustainability, as there isn't much regard for the bigger picture or personal impact.

Pull Leadership

Unlike the push leader, pull leaders are fantastic at building momentum, engaging their people along the way and proactively pulling people towards a specific vision. These are leaders who create engaging teams while still maintaining high standards that achieve real results. Pull leaders develop true partners in their team, engaging them in their roles in a way that allows them to show up with more of their talents, motivated to put them to use. Pull leaders see long-term results both for their overall organization and for their people.

A pull leader sees themselves as part of their team, encouraging future objectives to be built together and in a way that taps into what people want to do in their role. This leader approach often sees outside talent asking to be part of the team.

What's interesting about pull leadership is that it often feels very counterintuitive, since results may not be immediate. The pull style also appears to focus on development first, then results. In reality, results are always the focus; development is the long-term strategy for sustainable results.

Showing Up As A Pull Leader

Just as with anything new, showing up as a pull leader is about developing specific skills. Yes, there is going to be a bit of natural talent for some – whether it's an ability to listen or think of the bigger picture

– but magnetic leaders enhance their skills rather than relying solely on natural talents. Specifically, pull leaders are able to:

- **Influence:** You are able to help people see your thinking and understand it themselves, rather than forcing them to believe your idea. While this skill takes longer, when you're able to influence, you're able to get your team to do things because they understand *why* they're doing it, not just because you said so.

- **Define "Winning:"** Do your people actually know what they're working towards—what their "win" is going to be? Help your team identify what the long-term positive impacts of their work is, highlighting how they're actually winning in moving the company's purpose forward.

- **Delegate, Empower, and Trust:** When your people get the why behind the work, let them worry about the how. Empower and trust them to use their skills and have autonomy over the how. In doing this, you're helping them grow their mastery in their own expertise, fuelling their own fire for long-term growth. When you delegate, empower, and trust, you don't micromanage the talents out of people.

- **Balance People and Results:** You develop a balance between empathy for your people, alongside building boundaries and holding people accountable. As a leader, you're accountable for the growth of your people in addition to the results of your company. Pull leaders find this balance between relationships and achievements.

- **Be Authentic.** You are your most professional self, but you remain transparent and honest without oversharing. You have a sincere interest in people and genuinely show gratitude, coupled with confidence and humility.

- **Invest in Personal Development.** This demonstrates your ability to be vulnerable in knowing that you, as a leader, have more to learn. While this grows your development, you also quietly give permission to others to invest in their development, the definition of leading by example.

- **Be Emotionally Intelligent.** Pull leaders are not reactive stress baskets with stress oozing out of them. While you'll still have stress as a pull leader, you're better equipped to cope with this. In addition, part of your development is in listening to feedback, then implementing it. Emotionally intelligent leaders are able to do this without getting defensive or shutting down.

Ultimately, pull leadership leads to greater engagement, better balance between getting the work done—both with better results and relationships—and focuses on creating longer-term results that support not just the organization, but also the growth of your people. In the long-term, pull leadership is the easier path as it drives better quality results and employee engagement at the same time.

Imagine how pulling your people forward could transform your team.

DEVELOPING LEADERSHIP INFLUENCE IN YOUR INDUSTRY AND WITH YOUR TEAM

Imagine a prominent and respected leader. You might picture the leader of a team — that is, someone with direct reports — or perhaps a leader in a particular industry. These two types of leaders are not mutually exclusive.

So, what is the difference between being a leader in your industry and being a leader of a team? Do you have to choose between one or the other? If you want to be considered an effective and respected leader, which should you work toward first? It all depends on your current role and the type of leader you aspire to be.

Start With Self-Leadership

Self-leadership should always come first. You must develop into someone others can follow. Then, depending on your role, identify where to build out your leadership skills next. If you're leading a team, then start with effectively leading your team. If you have no direct reports, influencing leadership is likely your next step.

One is not necessarily more important than the other — both have value, and you can develop in either area. As a leadership and executive coach, I work with many clients who want to be more effective at leading direct reports, and part of that is being a trusted leader in your industry. You can work on becoming a leader in your industry even before you have direct reports. To be a leader in your industry is to cultivate a following through influence.

Growing As An Influential Leader When You Have Direct Reports

If you have direct reports, you owe it to them to have clear goals and a vision for the team's future. What are we working toward? These goals can be directly about what your team is working on, but influential leaders lead from a narrow view into a wider view beyond your organization. Consider working on industry goals with your team.

When you are a strong leader in your organization, you may be recognized as an industry leader as a result. Influence grows over time. It stems from an intentional choice to step up into good leadership. From there, reputation follows. Establishing a good reputation isn't something you work toward head-on — it's an added bonus, but certainly can't be your only goal.

What If You Do Not Have Direct Reports?

Even if you do not have a team to lead, anyone can choose to step into leadership. First, you must get involved in your community. Influential leadership shows up in many different areas and can help you build the necessary skill set to lead your own team today or in the future. Your community can exist within your local area, your industry or associations, in which you can develop different aspects of leadership.

If you are a founder of a startup or a new business owner, you may want to build your influence because leadership skills are often needed, even as a solo entrepreneur. For example, as a service provider, your clients expect you to guide them through your expertise. Leadership isn't just leading others; it's influencing others through your vision.

Your first step to influential leadership is asking, "What are you trying to achieve?" and leading them to achieve that goal.

What Goes Into Building Influential Leadership?

Becoming an influencing leader seems easier when you have direct reports because you are working from a position of authority. However, even if you don't have direct reports, the skills are the same.

There are several ways to develop your influential leadership skills:

- Network: Beyond meeting people at events and exchanging business cards, this should be all about building and developing deeper relationships and surrounding yourself with experts you will need or want help from at some point in your career.

- Have mentors and mentor others.

- Share your expertise: Speaking, writing articles, being a member of panels and thought leadership all grow your influence.

- Volunteer and contribute to your local community and industry.

- Dare to differ: Share an opinion and a vision that may not be what others expect.

Building Skills That Transcend Industries

Good leadership skills can take you across industries; if you prove yourself as an effective leader, you may be considered for a role in a different industry. Although most of the leaders I have worked with have stayed within the same industry throughout their career, I have worked with many who have been brought into executive roles in completely different fields from where they had built their career. Know that, even though you may not be an industry expert, you can find the right talent and experts to fill the necessary roles in your new organization. You can ensure that the experts are employing critical thinking and leading them into fully exploring options and information they might overlook, avoiding groupthink. Your role is to guide the experts around you to achieve common goals or fulfill that ultimate vision, not necessarily to become an industry expert yourself.

Should you find yourself transitioning to a leadership role in a new industry, take the early days to ask good questions, understand the industry, the company, the culture and the requirements of your role. Step back and listen. Create coalitions. Who are the key players you can surround yourself with? These are the foundations of influencing leadership that will help you be effective no matter what industry you're in.

The skill set behind self-leadership and influencing leadership, supported by management skills and a foundation of financial, HR, marketing and technology acumen, can prepare you for whatever comes your way. Developing your influencing leadership will not only help you become a more effective team leader, but it will also help you become a leader others want to follow whether they are direct reports, peers in the industry, clients, vendors or anyone who can help move your vision of the future forward. It doesn't matter where you start, it only matters that you start.

FOUR SKILLS YOU NEED
FOR COURAGEOUS LEADERSHIP

Reading, studying and talking about effective leadership is way easier than actually leading. Leadership is a space of no right answers, tough conversations, setting an unknown direction, influencing others and uncertain outcomes. Taking responsibility for the future of your business and the people in it carries a weight that can either lead us off course or can be harnessed into great outcomes.

Yet, no great outcome comes without missteps, disappointments, challenges and failures along the way. Leadership requires courage, and courage requires a special kind of vulnerability.

Based on the work of Dr. Brené Brown, as detailed in her book *Dare to Lead*, there are four skillsets for courageous leadership.

Rumbling With Vulnerability

As Brené Brown says, "You can't get to courage without rumbling with vulnerability." This means having the courage to show up fully when you can't control the outcome. It's about being vulnerable in your relationships with others in every meeting, email, phone call and face-to-face conversation inside and outside the workplace.

Vulnerability feels like being excited and afraid all at the same time. You feel you must do or say something, yet the inner voice you have tells you it might not be safe to do so. It takes vulnerability to delay action and step into a coaching conversation to help a team member find their own answers.

Leaders constantly need to work on stepping into tough conversations and providing honest and productive feedback, which requires this mindset. When it comes to providing feedback, remember the following:

- When you focus on clarity, you increase trust and decrease unproductive behavior. Being clear creates more connection and empathy. Clarity also creates a boundary that allows the other person to decide what to do with the feedback.

- Know your triggers. When you're triggered, do you try to control the situation, protect yourself or start people pleasing? Knowing this can help you move into a place of choice to step into vulnerability.

Living Your Values (Rather Than Simply Professing Them)

Get clear on what you believe and check that your intentions, words, thoughts and behaviors align with your beliefs. Name your values by writing them down. Then identify core behaviors that represent how you might live those values. And, what are the behaviors that tell you that you're off course?

Courageous leaders who live their values instead of just talking about them are never silent about hard things. For example, courageous leaders do not partake in willful blindness. As a leader, you must be aware of what is going on around you. You must realize when to act and know that sometimes you need to act in difficult situations. It takes courage to recognize these opportunities for leadership and to set an example for your team. Making decisions that honor your values will be tough because doing the right thing is rarely easy.

Braving Trust (And Being The First To Trust)

Now, I'm not advocating for blind trust, which is a combination of a high tendency to trust and/or no limited consideration. I'm talking about smart trust, which requires good business judgment and good people judgment combined to enhance your gut instinct and intuition.

Trust doesn't come before vulnerability. They actually go hand-in-hand. Trust is built through small moments of vulnerability in a relationship developed over time and also comes from choosing courage over comfort.

Being a trusting and trustworthy leader means being someone people can count on to do what you say you will do, including acting within your competencies and limitations. Own your mistakes and make amends. Accountability means that when there is a misstep, you're willing to ask yourself, "What part did I play in this?"

Stephen M.R. Covey, author of *The SPEED of Trust: The One Thing That Changes Everything,* tells us:

- In business, trust increases speed and thus decreases costs.

- Trust means confidence. You first have to trust yourself.

- Businesses should create value for others to cultivate societal trust.

Lastly, being vulnerable does not mean being a completely open book and taking down walls. On the contrary, setting boundaries for yourself and your team can help set an environment for trust.

Learning To Rise

How you talk to yourself when things go wrong matters a great deal. Ask Carol Dweck, author of the book *Mindset: The New Psychology of Success*. Looking for fault shows a fixed mindset; learning to become better the next time around shows a growth mindset. When something goes wrong, study the situation and find what is fact and what you are interpreting to fill in the blanks. Recognize the emotion that comes up for you, and get curious about it. Notice when one of the three most dangerous stories show up: those that diminish your worthiness, faith and creativity.

The most important aspect of courageous leadership is choosing how we respond to fear. Will you go autopilot and protect, control, or people please and appease?

Next time you're called upon to lead courageously, remember to "rumble with vulnerability" by showing up fully, living your values, being the first to trust and learning to rise when things don't go according to plan.

EMOTIONAL INTELLIGENCE

No doubt Emotional Intelligence is more rare than book smarts,
but my experience says that it is actually more important
in the making of a leader.

~ Jack Welch

I just need to find a way to take the emotion out of it. I've heard this many times from leaders I've worked with over the years and my answer is always the same – you can't. Leadership will always be uncomfortable; confidence comes from accepting this and developing the skills to find your way through the discomfort.

Emotional intelligence (EI) is the ability to include and even embrace emotions and use this information to guide your behaviour, decisions, and relationships. You can't lead people without recognizing their emotions, and the more you try, the more difficult it becomes. Leadership is a difficult role; you must also embrace your own emotions to have the best possible relationship with yourself.

Some of the benefits of developing EI include resilience and managing stress so that you maintain energy to bounce back when you encounter triggering situations. When others are losing their heads, you're able to keep calm and composed to make effective decisions and help others respond appropriately. Communicating in tough situations balances empathy, boundaries, and helps you maintain or even deepen relationships. You create fulfillment, ensuring you stay connected to purpose and goals that matter to you personally.

Emotional intelligence helps you navigate the uncertainty, ambiguity, and complexity of leadership. Embrace and include your emotions instead of excluding them.

NEW PERSPECTIVES ON LEADERSHIP LEARNED FROM A 1,200-POUND ANIMAL

It all started with wanting to lead a horse across a round pen — without a rope and with people all around. What felt like a potentially hokey scenario soon turned into one of the most transformational learning experiences I've had as a coach.

This experience was equine leadership coaching. Still considered an experiential leadership coaching technique, equine coaching is deeply personal as it focuses on the human-horse interaction, giving the individual insights solely into themselves, without human input. This perfectly lends itself to individuals brave enough to keep growing as leaders.

Leadership Lessons From Equine Coaching

You have to have the patience to see the whole picture.

When I first tried leading the horse, I thought it would be a quick process and we'd be walking throughout the round pen without a rope in no time.

I was wrong.

While I was able to get her to start following me, I soon learned that, in my hurry to lead, I didn't account for all of our surroundings. All other factors, including the other horses nearby, captivated my horse more than me and slowed our progress.

As leaders, when you take the time to slow down, get present and become aware of all factors and surroundings, you're able to proactively account for potential obstacles. Slow down to actually speed up your progress.

This nonjudgemental creature acts as your mirror.

As I led the horse, I noticed that whenever I hesitated, she hesitated. Whenever I looked back over my shoulder, she would stop. When I stopped looking for her and trusted she was there, she was there, following without question. Trust me, you know when a 1,200-pound animal is closing ground behind you.

What accounts for this change? It was simply my body language.

Equine coaching works because there is no judgment from the animal. Without the ability to verbally communicate, the horse relied on my body language for guidance. Since my body gave clues, I became more present and aware of what I was actually "saying." Here, I could find my blind spots and safely move through them. This place allowed me to challenge my beliefs and try something different in my approach where there are no real consequences should I fail. Through horses, I recognized the importance of leading from an authentic place.

People will follow you when they trust you.

When I worked through my blockages and led the horse with complete trust — no micromanaging of where she was, accounting for distractions along our route and leading without second-guessing myself — that horse followed me, connected with me and trusted me to safely guide her to our destination without a guiding rope. I'll never forget the feeling of the horse not only following me but her head coming up beside me as I confidently walked forward, trusting her to follow.

This transformation was not about getting on a horse and directly guiding it to what I wanted it to do. It was about the relationship with the horse and offering clarity on where I was going through my actions while standing on the ground. This is simple integrity that leads to building trust.

Show that you trust your people to follow, and they will trust you to lead.

Participate in the experience of leadership.

The trained equine leadership facilitator on the side of the corral guided me by asking questions. There was no real discussion in the moment, but there were questions that helped me focus on the full mind, body and, yes, even soul experience of leadership.

While equine coaching is about the relationship between you and the horse because it helps you work through your inner beliefs, the coach is there to help you notice subtle things you may be missing. They help you be more present, getting you out of your head (which is full of questions like "how am I going to lead this giant?" or "why isn't this horse following me") and into the experience of leading with awareness and intention.

Sure, we may have a plan for how we want things to go or how we think they are going to go, but this doesn't help us experience leadership as it's happening — nor does it let us lead with agility and trust in the moment.

For me, equine leadership coaching was the ultimate experiential leadership lab, accelerating my awareness of the impact of my thinking, beliefs and behaviors. It gave me an experimental place to try out new approaches and beliefs, helping me connect with my authentic leadership style. Whether you're looking to grow exponentially or fractionally, these may be the same types of insights you need. Are you brave enough to learn from a 1,200-pound animal?

EMOTIONALLY INTELLIGENT LEADERS DON'T SHUT OFF THEIR EMOTIONS—THEY MANAGE THEM

Business decision, most senior leaders have probably been told to "just take the emotion out of it." But there's a lot more to this advice than simply turning off your emotions.

Emotional intelligence, also known as EQ, is the ability to recognize emotions and effectively manage them not only toward others but toward one's self. Emotionally intelligent leaders know that every decision they make does have emotions tied to them, but it's how you manage those emotions that matters.

Research shows that successful leaders already tend to have higher EQ compared to the general population. It is a critical competency, especially for senior leaders, and it is difficult to be an effective leader without development in this area.

EQ As Part Of The Leadership Skillset

Some of the assessments that I use with my clients when we first start working together are around EQ: the EQ-i 2.0, from Reuven Bar-On and Multi-Health Systems, and the Emotional and Social Competency Inventory (ESCI) 360° assessment by Korn Ferry and Daniel Goleman.

Both models highlight some of the concepts that are overlooked as critical EQ skills for leaders. Many EQ tests or frameworks evaluate motivation, empathy and social skills, which tend to be more outward-facing. The EQ-i 2.0 model includes stress management and decision-making as equally important factors. Leaders need to be flexible, optimistic and tolerant to stress. They also need to be able to solve problems and remain objective, resisting rash decisions driven by emotion. The ESCI model highlights emotional self-awareness and self-management. Leaders with high EQ are aware of their emotions and are able to manage them in their everyday dealings.

These are just two validated tools that help measure a leader's EQ. Even more important is working with leaders to debrief on the results of these assessments to identify gaps and follow through by creating development. Unlike personality assessments that might measure preferences (i.e., who you already are), EQ evaluations are development tools because EQ changes over time. It's not something that you either have or you don't—it's something you can continually work on and progress.

The perception is that some leaders just have higher EQ than others, but it's not an innate skill or trait. Rather, it is something that they have learned throughout their life experiences. That might be why there is a belief that women leaders have higher EQ than male leaders. Growing up, men may be subjected to different EQ-developing situations compared to women, but that could be applied to anyone regardless of gender. To this point, your environment and your learning opportunities have played a part in your personal EQ development.

EQ At Work

At any given moment, a leader will need to leverage their EQ. Think about having to deal with a public situation where your employees may have competing political opinions on an issue, or conflicting viewpoints leading to stakeholder pressure. Any leader in any industry can probably think of a situation that fits this scenario. You will likely need to draw on the following skills:

- Stress tolerance, because the situation is difficult to navigate.

- Empathy, to recognize and understand how others feel.

- Reality testing, listening and posing reflecting questions to push biases aside.

- Decision-making, and standing by that decision but being open to future information that could change it.

Teams may also need to learn about their own EQ and how that affects how they work with each other. Often teams will simply do the work and not look at EQ concepts that impact team dynamic. Top leadership teams that work closely together should consider EQ assessments. After all, EQ can pervade the whole organization, and it starts from the top.

Applying EQ To Your Leadership

The important thing to remember is that EQ is not about lovey-dovey, warm-and-fuzzy feelings. You can be your own style of leader but build upon the gaps in your EQ skillset to better manage your emotions—that's why it's worth looking into assessments. What's underneath the feedback? And what is the root cause of the areas needing improvement?

One leader I work with studied his assessment and glossed over the positives but took the negatives hard. His employees raved about his social skills but they felt that he did not provide feedback strongly enough. He was high in empathy, but lower in assertiveness—another key element of high EQ. Improving his assertiveness did not mean that he had to become less empathetic. Rather, he could draw on this strength to be more assertive in providing constructive feedback.

Another leader I coached received feedback saying she was too assertive. Her position was in a highly safety-sensitive environment, and employees felt that she did not come across as if she cared when talking to them. She was high in assertiveness and lower on empathy, but she did care deeply about employee safety—that's why she was doing what she was doing. She gained awareness about how she could be more assertive in showing how she cared about others.

The bottom line: You don't have to change who you are to become a more emotionally intelligent, more effective leader.

Flexing Your EQ Muscles

The wonderful thing about EQ is that you can always keep working on it. There are a lot of useful resources that provide coping skills and practices specifically designed to help leaders. Books like *The EQ Edge: Emotional Intelligence and Your Success* by Steven J. Stein and Howard E. Book have self-assignments that you can apply to difficult leadership situations.

When you "take the emotion out of it" and ignore your emotions, you're ignoring critical information. It's just as bad as being completely driven by your emotions. Developing your EQ provides new perspectives. Your awareness of your own strengths will let you build upon them, identify and fill gaps and become a highly emotionally intelligent leader.

HOW LEADERS CAN SHARE TOUGH NEWS EFFECTIVELY AND WITH EMPATHY

The burden of sharing tough news is unfortunately part of being a leader. No matter how long your career, sharing tough news never gets easier. But even though being the bearer of bad news is tough on the messenger, it's always tougher on the person who's on the receiving end. This is why sharing tough news with clarity and heart is an essential skill for any leader.

Why sharing tough news is difficult

When we have tough news to share, we are most often afraid of the reaction of the person (or people) upon delivering the message. What if they cry? What if they shut down and it's awkward? What if they get mad? And if any of the above happens, then what? What if I change my decision and start to backpedal?

Upon receiving a reaction, we may try to overcorrect and not respond appropriately, unsure how to handle the situation. We may try to soften the blow and, as a result, become indirect and wrap a story around the actual news. The recipient of the news might become confused and not truly understand what you are actually saying. That is why the kind thing to do is to always be clear when sharing tough news.

Sharing Tough News With Clarity

A common example is having to deliver the news of company layoffs. A company might send out a mass email with the following message:

"We had to say goodbye to 25 employees."

This might seem like a nicer way to put things, but it is unclear what is actually happening to the employees. Were they laid off? Furloughed? Reassigned? Here's a better way to start:

"We've had to lay off 25 employees."

This is a clear statement that provides understanding. Often when we deliver tough news, the recipient may not immediately grasp the news. You may need to repeat it to them, and to others, so they can process the information. When you try and soften the news, talk in circles or provide unnecessary details, they can't hear or process your key points. When you deliver tough news, you need to help the recipient hear and understand what you are saying. Now is not the time for rationalizing, examining the big picture or explaining detailed next steps.

There are three questions to answer in your delivery of tough news:

1. What? This is the simplest one-line message of the news.

2. So what? This is what this news means to the listener or the impact on the listener.

3. Now what? This is what the listener can expect going forward.

How To Bring In Empathy When Sharing Tough News

The best model for delivering tough news is SPIKES, a six-step process developed by researchers for use in the healthcare industry. Here's how it applies to a work environment:

Setting Up

This first step is all about preparation. Find the right environment to deliver tough news, which depends on the context. If it impacts one person, it should be one-to-one. If it impacts a team, then it could be in a team meeting. Other times it might impact the team but be more appropriate to tell each person one-to-one first and then have a team meeting. We must also prepare the leadership team so that they have a unified message, especially when the news affects the entire organization.

Perception

What do you know about the receiver's current state of mind? What is their experience when it comes to these things? This is where you step into empathy. What might they already know about the news you are about to deliver? Perhaps you have alluded to details in a previous memo or meeting that led to the decision made. How have they been responding to the information thus far?

Invitation

Delivering tough news with empathy also means being conscious of whether the recipient might be ready to receive the news. Ask for permission to share the news. Sometimes this is implied by an invitation to a meeting about the topic. Asking for permission signals respect.

Knowledge

Prepare how you'll give them a heads up that there will be tough news coming their way. Saying something like "I have hard news to share with you today" may help the recipient prepare themselves for the news.

Emotions And Empathy

Prepare for the emotions that will come up for them and for you. While you are delivering the news, it can't be about you. And you can be surprised about what comes up. Consider how you will respond with kindness and care. First, you need to process your own feelings about the news so you can deliver it clearly. Perhaps you might need to journal or talk it out with another person. Sometimes when we are given bad news to deliver, we won't always have that much time to do this. Something as simple as going into a quiet room to collect yourself will go a long way.

Strategy

This is where you can start to consider the next steps and outline the move-forward plan, providing the recipient with some amount of certainty. In the case where you are laying off an employee, this might mean talking about the severance package. For the team not being laid off, it may mean telling them about how the change might affect their roles or duties in the near term.

We talk too much when we give tough news, when really we need to keep it simple. When people receive tough news, their limbic brain takes over. Your job is to help them process. Whether they cry, get mad or shut down, by following the above steps and preparing yourself beforehand, you will be able to deliver tough news with clarity and heart.

Delivering tough news is not easy, so be good to yourself too. Give yourself what you give to others. Practice self-compassion, both before sharing the news and after.

THE PORT IN THE STORM: WHAT LEADERS CAN DO TO KEEP CALM IN A CRISIS

For senior leaders, dealing with a crisis is not a matter of if, but when. Whether large or small, internal or external, a crisis can test a leader and their team. If you are a leader of a large organization, there is a chance that a crisis would have had to escalate to an extent before it comes to you. Because of this, executives might feel like they should just jump in and fix whatever the issue is. However, it is important to remember that it is not all up to you. You don't always have to have the right answer.

While there are other aspects of crisis management such as preparing your public relations, human resources or legal departments, I want to explore what leaders can personally do to keep calm in a crisis:

The First Encounter

When first presented with a crisis, your initial reaction will set the tone for how you feel about the issue at hand and, therefore, how you react to it. The key is to slow down. When I think about senior leaders managing their reactions to a major crisis, I often think about how President George W. Bush maintained his composure upon first learning of the events on 9/11. According to *Harvard Business Review*, crisis consultant Tim Johnson wrote that President Bush "bought himself space to think and time to react."

To steady yourself, try one or both of the following microhabits:

- Take a breath. Slow down even just for a moment to respond rather than react.

- Think to yourself, "How fascinating." Even the simple act of thinking this phrase helps reframe our mindset to first ask questions and be curious about the issue, instead of triggering a reaction.

Ask questions and get more detail. For example, you might say: "Tell me more," "Help me understand," "What is the impact we know about?" or "What are the risks?" When everyone else is speeding up and freaking out around you, you need to slow down so you can make conscious, deliberate decisions and not react out of fear.

Steadying Your Team And Your Organization

Reach out to key advisors and supports. Consider the right thing to do through the lens of your organizational values, personal values and moral ethics. Imagine the long-term implications of the decisions, not just the immediate impacts. Making short-term decisions might ease the situation, but it can prolong the crisis.

To steady your team, acknowledge the emotions everyone is experiencing. When you ask your team to "push through" without recognizing the emotions they are dealing with, they'll be more reactive. Make it safe to feel how they feel.

While others might tell you to remain positive in a crisis, it is inauthentic and hard to believe. Be honest without scaring people. If things are bad, explain the situation honestly, and don't promise everything will be fine unless you know for certain that it will be. (Hint: we never really know!) Instead, share your belief that the team will find its way through the crisis together.

Communicate early and often, even if you don't have all the information. Share what you know about the crisis, what you're doing and what might be next. Provide regular updates even if nothing has changed. Be honest, and don't gloss over tough information.

Using Emotional Intelligence In Crisis Management

Emotional management is key to establishing the direction that your organization needs to go to get through the crisis. When people talk about steady leadership, the metaphor of a port in a storm is often used. But what we need to remember about this metaphor is this: The lighthouse itself does not bring boats in. The lighthouse operator cannot see the rocks in the water; the captains of the boats out on the water can.

In the same vein, an executive can provide a steadying light for teams and organizations in a crisis, but they can't do it alone. You are not the hero or savior; you play an important role, but you have to be able to trust and empower your team to work together through the crisis. Crisis management is organizationwide, and part of it must come before a crisis even hits. Work with your leaders through potential scenarios to empower them to make decisions during a crisis, even before it is escalated to the executive level. This is an essential component of company culture: how you make decisions to deal with crises that come.

Self-Care During A Crisis

It's easy to let go of all self-care while you're working through a crisis, but it's critical to step away and take breaks for sleeping, eating, connecting with family and mentally recharging. Depending on the crisis, you might not be getting a full night's sleep every night, but it does need to be at least a few hours. This will help you recharge so you can think clearly, make key decisions and communicate effectively as you lead through the crisis. No one is effective after 24 hours with no sleep and living on donuts and coffee.

Some crises extend far beyond the initial event. For example, a mayor dealing with a major catastrophe, such as a fire or flood, will have to deal with issues for months, if not years. Prolonged exposure to the crisis can lead to long-term mental health impacts. Even when it's all over, it can take a while to return from a heightened crisis alert mode to a new business normal. It's important to keep boundaries around self-care, exercise, unplugging and healthy eating. Also, consider speaking with a mental health professional or engaging the support of a coach to help you work through the mental and emotional burden that crises bring.

In a crisis, you are managing yourself as well as your team. Remember that you are not the hero or the savior, but you play an important role. Trust must flow both ways between you and your team so that you can navigate the crisis together.

MANAGING TRIGGERS UNDER STRESS

We all face varying degrees of stress from different sources in our daily lives. As much as we try, we are not always able to prevent the stress in our personal life from affecting our professional life, and vice versa. As you move up in your career into senior management and executive leadership, you may feel added pressures in your role, and the way you deal with stress can have a wider impact on the people around you.

Stress Triggers Can Come In Many Forms

Stress is a sudden state of overwhelm, sadness, anxiety or panic. It can cause feelings of being devalued, disempowered or disgraced. It may seem like your energy has been drained, and you may feel powerless, stuck, confused or disoriented, frustrated or angry or generally not good enough.

Stress triggers are unique to each person because stress comes from life events that we perceive as negative for us. We all have a lot to juggle. Something that might not have been a big deal last week could become the straw that breaks the camel's back today. Stress-inducing events may include:

- Receiving difficult news
- An increased sense of responsibility or pressure

- Feeling burned out and overworked and being asked to take on more

- Comments or experiences where we feel judged

- Conflict with someone

- Feeling emotionally or physically unsafe

- Experiencing change and/or uncertainty

How Stress Affects Our Behavior

When our bodies feel stress, we typically react in one of three ways: fight, flight or freeze. This is because we can't physically think in these moments, as our limbic brain, also referred to as the lizard brain, takes over and prioritizes all functions to our survival.

Our behaviors toward other people are also deeply affected in times of stress. Dr. Linda Hartling adapted research from psychoanalyst Karen Horney and expanded on these three responses to stress, indicating that our behavioral responses fall into one of three patterns: protect (move away), comply (move toward/people please) and control (move against).

When we are triggered by stress, we ultimately try to create safety for ourselves by doubling down on our strengths that normally create success, using them in unhealthy ways.

When we protect, we may shut down and become unable to interact with others. We may even become critical, or use cynicism and sarcasm. We lob subtle attacks from a distance.

When we comply, we become overly people-pleasing to the point that we compromise on our own beliefs and feelings just to end the conflict, including getting overly focused on rules, and become overly passive or passive-aggressive.

When we control, we may lash out and say something we later regret, verbally attack or get physically violent.

While all three responses create short-term safety for us, they ultimately erode our relationships with others. Afterward, we may feel guilt or shame about how we reacted to the conflict. It's important to remember that these responses come from the limbic brain making quick and impulsive decisions, as opposed to the rational brain.

We Can't Avoid Stress, But We Can Reduce Our Resulting Behaviors

It is difficult to respond to stressful situations when you are already stressed, which is why it is important to look back on how you ended up in the situation. Reflect on your behaviors. Get to know how you typically respond to stress, then work backward to understand some of the moments that occurred just before the behavior. What happened? What did you or someone else say? What were you thinking and feeling? What were you feeling in your body? Did your breathing change? Did you tense up? Experience tunnel vision? Did your chest get tight or your throat constrict?

You can't avoid getting triggered, but you can avoid falling down a slippery slope. Watch for early warning signs. Without awareness, you can't identify the tools you need to address your triggers.

First, take deep breaths—counting helps you use your rational brain. Focus on something small. When going into a meeting where you might receive difficult news, prepare yourself. When you see early warning signs, take a break. Remember that you can always leave a conversation and come back when you've had a chance to process your thoughts and feelings. You can ask for a moment to regroup, but don't walk away completely from the situation. Just know that if you are the one to leave, the accountability is on you to return. When you come back, your ability to reengage is improved with a more rational, prepared mind.

Dealing With Stress Starts With Taking Care Of You

You're not fit for optimal human interaction when you're stressed. To lessen the burden in your life and prevent overwhelm, you must do things that help you recharge. Talk with someone about your feelings—a loved one, a close friend or colleague or a coach or therapist. Undertake activities to recharge, like meditation, exercise, rest, journaling, listening to music and so on.

For example, I work with one client who needs a meaningful goal in place to give him purpose and direction in order to manage work and life stress effectively. He found himself unable to get motivated for triathlon training when his races got canceled. So we worked together to reframe how he could find something he could control and set an attainable goal to motivate him. He spoke with his triathlon coach, who helped him organize ways to beat his own records (by achieving a personal best) and compete with others (by sharing their training times).

The most important way to take care of yourself and manage stress is to practice self-compassion. Treat yourself the way you would treat a friend under stress. Instead of dwelling on how you responded to a stressful situation, be kind to yourself and reserve judgment. We can't always change the past, but we can try to control how we respond in the future.

HOW TO FIND FULFILLMENT
AS A LEADER

When we talk about mental health, a work-life balance almost always comes up. I understand the intention, but I struggle with the word "balance" because to me, it implies a comparison. You are the only person who can identify what balance is for yourself. Yet, I've found that many leaders feel out of balance and tell themselves it's OK and they're happy with things (when they're not). What feels balanced to you might not work for someone else, so the first step is understanding what makes you feel fulfilled.

You must first establish a strong mindset as the foundation of who you are as a leader. This is a journey that requires a lot of internal work before determining the external skills and tactics of leadership—how we interact with others and take actions to achieve team and organizational goals. Without this mindset, the skills and tactics don't have a solid foundation to create the greatest impact.

Know who you are and what fulfills you.

The key to better mental health as a leader is fulfillment, which enables you to be effective in your organization and be better for the people around you outside of your corporate role.

To understand what fulfills you, start by getting to know yourself. Personal reflection is good, but a 360-degree assessment and feedback might help you get really clear on who you are. Someone like a coach, therapist, mentor or peer can give further insight into your true self that you might not be able to reach on your own.

Senior leadership can take its toll on your health and personal life if you don't have a strong mindset and understanding of yourself. What are your values? What are your personal priorities? Who are the important people in your life? Knowing these can help you make decisions regarding balance that are unique to you that leave you feeling fulfilled, even if you have a lot on your plate.

Practice self-care in the corporate world.

I've observed that promoting mental health in the corporate world seems to be on an upward trend with much discussion about psychologically healthy workplaces, employee and family assistance (EFAP) programs, wellness programs and the like. While executives encourage and support their employees taking part, they often fail to model it by doing so for themselves.

I work with many executives who struggle with saying "no" because they're dedicated to serving their company and their team. I've had clients who go a full day without eating or even going to the bathroom. They're up late at night and find they are neglecting their family, their marriages and their own self-care. Consider the following:

- Do you find yourself doing what you most value or what is important to you?

- Do you pursue personal or professional learning and growth?

- Do you have opportunities for play and leisure?

- Do you engage in reflection or other mindfulness activities?

- Do you struggle to set boundaries?

- Are you present mentally and emotionally with those you care about?

- Do you attend to your own personal physical care, such as diet and exercise?

Recognize that every "yes" requires a "no" to something else. Are you unconsciously saying no to your family, your own interests and goals, your own personal care? Ask yourself this question: "For every 'yes,' what am I saying 'no' to?" When you put 100% of your focus on others and 0% on yourself, you cannot be strategic, emotionally resilient or present for the people that you care about.

Leaders who take time for themselves show their employees that it's good to do the same. Take time for personal reflection. Block out time to prepare for meetings or work on strategic projects. Block out your vacations. I have one client who has five weeks of vacation each year, as well as four weeks of accrued vacation. This is why it's critical to plan your time off. By scheduling vacation time for the entire year, you can say "no" to other commitments and take the time needed to be with your family and recharge. You shouldn't need the first six days of a ten-day vacation to de-stress.

Lead with empathy and understanding.

Empathy without boundaries isn't empathy, it's sympathy. Empathy is about understanding how someone feels and communicating it to the other person to check your understanding. When you say, "I know we're all struggling with this decision," it might seem inauthentic; you are implying that you are trying to put yourself in their shoes when you cannot truly understand their perspective. Instead, you can say, "I know I am struggling with this decision, and I feel you might be too. I am here to support you." This is a much more human response and shows them that it is OK to have difficulty surrounding the situation. It also keeps your boundaries in place.

Empathy doesn't mean you rescue the other person from their feelings or change your decision to make them feel better. In my experience, when you abandon self-compassion to take on sympathy and rescuing others, you become a martyr and begin to feel resentment towards the other person.

Lastly, when you begin changing your behaviors to find fulfillment and balance that works for you, make sure to communicate these changes with the people around you. Explain to your team why you are setting strict availability times so that you can have dedicated personal time. If you are volunteering after work hours, sit down with your loved ones and tell them why this other opportunity means so much to you. Having open communication around this change shows the congruence between your behavior and your words.

By looking inward first, getting to know yourself and determining what fulfills you, you will be better equipped to make decisions that help you achieve balance—whatever that looks like to you. Then, opening lines of communication between yourself and the people around you will help you find fulfillment in your role and beyond.

BOUNDARIES & CHOICE

You get what you create, and you get what you allow.

~ Dr. Henry Cloud

I'm fascinated by choice. Even when we feel we have no choice, we always do: our outlook and attitude in any moment. I'm also a big believer that there is no such thing as time management, only choice management.

It's easy to fall into the comfortable, default reactive thought and behaviour patterns that have served you well up to this point in your career. Leaders who excel in both relationships and achieving long-term results pause and reflect on their choices before making them. Getting absolutely clear on what you want is the first step; the second is challenging your perception of your part in getting to the desired outcome.

Boundaries are a form of choice. They start with considering what is OK and not OK for your behaviour and the behaviour of others when interacting with you, the team, your clients, and stakeholders. Boundaries also include challenging decisions such as deciding when something has reached its end, even if it's difficult, or when allowing others to own their part of the relationship, including permitting them to fail so they can learn, clean up, and try again.

Team and organizational norms and values are critical in healthy boundaries. Boundaries can often be overstepped, intentionally and unintentionally; choosing to talk through these tough moments can help you refine boundaries and set new ones.

What are you choosing?

THE ROLE THAT BOUNDARIES PLAY IN LEADERSHIP GROWTH

Setting boundaries is a major part of any leader's skill set. Many leaders are aware of the habits that they need to work on to enforce boundaries, such as unplugging from work, taking vacation time or even committing to only the tasks you have time or capacity for and delegating the rest.

However, there are other instances in the workplace where we might not realize that we need to set our own boundaries or avoid crossing the boundaries of our coworkers.

Setting boundaries means setting precedents.

Boundaries, in short terms, define what's OK and what's not OK. It's the fence between you and others—where I begin and you end. As Dr. Henry Cloud highlights in *Boundaries for Leaders: Results, Relationships, and Being Ridiculously in Charge*, "You get what you create and you get what you allow." This is especially true in the workplace.

One common example is working overtime. When we constantly work 10-12 hours a day or respond to emails on evenings and weekends, it sets a precedent that we're always on. Occasionally you may need to work some overtime, but you would need to enforce that boundary to show when that's OK for you and when it's not.

Another type of boundary we might not realize we need to set is a self-enforced boundary around our responsibilities. Sometimes we work with our heads down and get so caught up in our day-to-day that we might start not only owning certain responsibilities but essentially building an empire around our role. Or we become known for doing certain things so our team members default to us owning them and don't want to learn how to do them because we're "so good" at it.

One of my clients is a great example of this. A professional with several years of experience, she's also the youngest member of her team. Because of this, taking notes at meetings became her responsibility and one that she took seriously. But it got to the point where she would spend so much time editing and perfecting the notes that it took time away from her being able to actually execute essential tasks that she had built her skills and training upon. She had to learn to set a boundary with her team and with herself that she should only dedicate a set amount of time and effort on these notes so that she could get to more important, strategic work. To paraphrase Dale Carnegie, decide how much time and energy something is worth and refuse to give it more.

When we own certain responsibilities to the point of not sharing the load with the team, we can also pigeonhole ourselves and block our own career growth. It can set a precedent with senior leadership who might see you only in that role. This is a relatively common scenario. You can become so irreplaceable in that job, that they see promoting you as a risk because you would create a vacuum in your current role. Instead, they would rather hire someone above you. That can be the death of a career. But realizing this and setting and enforcing a boundary with yourself can help avoid this situation.

You also have to accept the consequences of boundaries.

When leaders move up the career ladder to senior and executive roles, they might not realize that they will have increased demands on their time and attention from other people in the organization to solve problems. That's why it's especially important to set and enforce boundaries with others, but also respect others' boundaries.

Boundary enforcement is certainly difficult as a leader. What makes it even harder is that enforcing boundaries may disappoint people. But at this level, leaders cannot focus on making everybody happy all the time.

On the other hand, if leaders try to make decisions based on how they think other people will react, they essentially cross the boundaries of the other party because they've tried to save them from their emotions instead of owning their problems. Remember: Boundaries are where I begin and you end. All you can do is show up composed and respectful and try not to control how the other party reacts. They don't need protection—they need you to show up in your role.

Boundaries build trust.

Boundaries are an essential element of trust. When you have no boundaries, it leaves the other person guessing what the guardrails are in their relationship or interaction with you and they wonder whether they are going too far. We have more trust in those who help us by articulating the guardrails. When we have no boundaries, we also set the unspoken expectation that others cannot have boundaries with us.

In the workplace, leaders need to set an example for others to follow when it comes to setting and enforcing boundaries. When you don't say no to your teammates or direct reports, they might not feel safe to say no to you. When employees feel safe to enforce boundaries with their leader, they can be more transparent when negotiating boundaries to get results.

Think about discussing limits and capacity. When an employee says, "I can only work on these two projects in this timeframe," leaders can be assured that the projects will be done well because they're not taking too much on. Leaders should also make decisions to manage other resources across the organization so work can still be done. If there's too much work to spread around, there may be a business case for a new full-time employee. But this conversation starts with a conversation around boundaries.

Boundaries are only effective when we set and enforce them with ourselves and others. These are the rules, and we have to be willing to accept the consequences of enforcing them, because the consequences are far greater than when we don't. We are not a victim of our circumstances. Boundaries give us the power to choose and the responsibility to decide.

IS YOUR OPEN DOOR POLICY HURTING YOU AS A LEADER?

Open door policies are great in theory, but could they actually be making you a less respected or effective leader?

The Tale Of The Open Door Fail

I used to meet with a client in his office. When we would close the door for our sessions, not one moment would go by without his team knocking on the door, interrupting the work we were doing to build his leadership qualities.

So why did his team think it was OK to interrupt his personal development time? Because he never set boundaries. His open door policy was 24/7, and he was constantly being pulled away from his priorities. If you don't set clear boundaries as to when you are OK with being available versus when you're not, you will constantly be pulled away from important tasks.

It's true that as a leader, you want to be available to your team, supporting them in whatever manner they need. However, by always being available, you are hindering, not developing, your team. To be a strong leader, you must first make time for your priorities to support your company's overall goals. As a result, you must create boundaries. As Brené Brown highlights, leaders who have boundaries are ultimately more effective and compassionate.

No Boundaries? No Trust

If you are always reacting to putting out fires and solving your team's problems, you aren't establishing your priorities with them. By clearly identifying what you are and are not OK with, your team is clear about when they should come to you versus trying to problem solve on their own. If you don't establish boundaries, you are doing a disservice to both you and your team because:

- You aren't supporting their critical thinking growth.

- You are demonstrating that you aren't enforcing boundaries yourself and that you might expect the same from them.

- You aren't delivering quality work.

- You are burnt out and may resent your team because they rely on you to solve their problems.

- You remain in a reactive mindset because you are saying yes to everyone.

As Dr. Henry Cloud highlights in *Boundaries for Leaders: Results, Relationships, and Being Ridiculously in Charge*, "You get what you create and you get what you allow." Meaning, if you talk about your boundaries, but don't enforce them, it's like calling wolf. Your team respects you less because you don't do what you say you're going to do. Your team knows that your boundaries can be broken, so they'll break them.

While an open door policy isn't bad, it is crucial that you set specific boundaries to be supportive and compassionate towards your team, while still completing the requirements of your role, such as strategic thinking initiatives.

When you enforce boundaries, you have better relationships, as you set aside dedicated time to support your team along with other members of your organization. This allows you to be intentional with your conversations while teaching others to be more purposeful in coming to you if they truly need your advice.

Understanding Your Boundaries

While talking about boundaries is great, how do you start to define and practice yours?

1. Identify your values and priorities.

By clearly identifying your values, particularly in a challenging situation, you get clear on what you should say yes or no to. This allows you to keep your integrity in a tough situation because you are doing exactly what you have said you're going to do.

2. Recognize that you can't be liked at all times.

You're a leader, not a best friend, so you will disappoint people when you say no. Just know that in these moments of saying no, you're actually supporting your team member's growth, encouraging them to use their own skills and tools to solve a problem, and allowing them to trust their own instincts. You're helping people refocus their attention on what matters most for both you and them.

3. Set boundaries at work and home.

Your home and work life shouldn't overly invade each other, even if your role is such that there aren't set hours. For example, when having dinner with your family, set the boundary that you will not answer phone calls or emails. This allows you to be engaged in the moment. Hiccups happen, but don't allow them to become the norm.

4. Expect your boundaries to be violated.

People are human and they'll make mistakes, testing your boundaries as you start to enforce them. However, it's important to remember that a lack of preparedness on someone else's part does not constitute an emergency on yours. This doesn't mean you're not compassionate toward their problem, it simply means that you're helping them grow in understanding how to better prepare.

5. Lead by example.

Having integrity means that you're walking your talk. If you encourage your team members to have boundaries, but you don't, they won't feel like they really can. Look at what your actions are saying in relation to your boundaries.

Once you're able to identify what your personal boundaries are, you're able to define clear expectations with others. Have an open door policy, but be clear about what your personal policy is. With these well defined, you'll build a more resourceful team, allowing you to be a more effective leader.

BEING A LIKEABLE LEADER DOESN'T MEAN BEING LIKED ALL THE TIME

It's natural, even instinctive, to want to be liked. We're social beings and connection is essential to human survival. We want to be wanted. We want to be trusted and relied on. Being a leader is very much about being connected with people.

Many leaders reached their position because they were exceptional at bringing people together, inspiring, growing and developing others and building loyalty with team members and customers. They've often been great rescuers; they're the keen listeners who help others solve problems and make their lives easier. However, being a leader also means making decisions and having tough conversations that may lead to moments in which you aren't liked by everyone.

Let go of the need to be liked.

To like someone means you find them agreeable, enjoyable or satisfactory. To respect is to hold feelings of deep admiration for someone because of their abilities, qualities or achievements. But being respected does not mean you have to be liked and vice versa. You can admire and accept a leader whom you may not find agreeable because you see the consistency and conviction of their values and fair treatment. In other words, they do the "right thing."

The desire to be liked, all the time, at all costs, cannot be fulfilled when you are a leader. Some people feel that if they're not liked all the time, that they're not likeable at all—and that's not true. In a leadership role, you encounter situations when you know that what you're about to do won't make people like you in the moment but will lead to earning their respect.

In Dr. Brené Brown's book *Braving the Wilderness*, she argues that to truly belong you have to be able to stand alone. This is especially true for leaders. You need to have something to stand for. When you attach your identity as a leader to being liked at all costs, you prioritize meeting everyone's expectations. You avoid conflict for the sake of artificial harmony. You may start to water down your vision and lose your personal aspirations. You may struggle with change or innovation and avoid setting big, audacious goals. When you lead, you need to be able to stand up for your values even when it means not being liked.

Respectable leaders are consistent in their approach, interested in people and committed to their growth. They are compassionate and have boundaries. They're focused on people and achieving great things together and share accountability and responsibility. For example, when mentoring someone, will you share difficult feedback with them for the sake of their growth even if it may be hard for them to hear? Will you share it even if they may not like you today, with hopes that in the future they'll see you were invested enough in them to share hard things no one else would?

Get comfortable being uncomfortable.

It's never easy to make tough calls. I've worked with leaders who have asked me when making hard decisions would become more comfortable. The answer? Never. The work, and especially the relationships, are important to you, so you care. And that's why it's uncomfortable. But you have to care enough about other people to be candid and honest with them about why you made those decisions.

Leaders must navigate these tough calls from a place of "why." Reflect on your values, the organization's values and the outcome you're trying to reach by making the difficult decision. Talk with someone on your support team—maybe your peers, boss or coach—beforehand to get clear on this. Then, share the why when communicating your decision—not to convince your audience but to help them understand despite the discomfort.

A leader I once worked with had to make a tough decision, but when employees and stakeholders tried to talk to him about it, he chose not to entertain them—not because he didn't want to listen, but because he feared that he would be swayed into changing his mind. If you're confident in your decision and have thought it through, you're unlikely to change your mind. Listening doesn't mean you have to agree or do what they want. You can explain your decision and that you considered all the information you had when you made it. People don't have to like it, but they can respect how you got to it.

At the same time, you don't have to hustle and convince people to like your decision. If they have to respect your decision, you have to respect the fact that they may disagree with it. Otherwise, you are overstepping their boundaries, robbing them of learning and growing and simply trying to fulfill your need to be liked.

Stand for your convictions.

Leadership is about challenge, having a vision and taking steps toward the future. You will always have competing stakeholders, and they won't be agreeable all the time. Tough calls can be a gift for leaders: They represent an opportunity to seize the moment, take action and gain respect with a decision based on core values. When you communicate your decision with empathy, most people around you will recognize that it was a difficult decision and credit you for being an authentic and inspired leader.

Remember: Tricky situations will be made easier if you pause to reflect on your intentions and gain clarity and conviction with your coach or trusted thought partner. Whenever you make a hard decision, there will be people who won't like you for it, and there will always be outliers regardless of how "good" your decision is for the organization. Trying to please everyone ends up pleasing no one. If you're bound to disappoint someone all the time, be sure that you're not disappointing yourself.

REBUILDING YOUR AUTHORITY WHEN YOUR LEADERSHIP IS OVERSTEPPED

You're a leader. You're responsible for specific decisions, strategy and outcomes that impact your company. Chances are, you have your team who supports you, but you most likely also have a senior leader or governing body, such as a board of directors, who you report to. And sometimes, these senior leaders may overstep and tell you what to do, rather than stay within their role of governance.

More often than not, this isn't being done intentionally. Rather, this may be because there isn't clarity on everyone's respective roles, it's unclear as to what you're asking or your confidence as a leader hasn't been demonstrated to your senior leaders.

How, then, do you establish this authority to avoid having your leadership overstepped?

Establish Boundaries For Clarity

If the scope of your role is not clearly defined, the chances for overstepping your leadership is heightened. Ensure that you and your board have clearly defined the scope of your role, decision-making and accountabilities.

For example, you may have a budget allowance where you are allowed to spend up to a specific amount without requiring permission from the board. Should you require a higher budget, then you need to run this by the board to spend this specific amount.

Have conversations regarding where you have authority to just act versus where you require support for decision-making. With your board, take the time to educate each other on individual authorities (e.g., the board's role is leadership strategy, the big picture, holding the CEO accountable, etc., while your operational leader role guides *how* the work gets done to support the larger governance pieces of the board).

This will help establish clear boundaries to better define the rules of engagement and decision-making moving forward.

Note Whether You Are A Permission Seeker Or Authority Builder

When reaching out to your senior leader, note whether you're asking for permission or looking for feedback. How you frame your presentation may invite overstepping by your leader. If asking for approval, they may jump into solution and decision-making mode. Whereas, if you present an update, you demonstrate your authority as a leader, increasing the board's confidence in your abilities.

For instance, rather than saying "I'd like your feedback on my approach," be more assertive, stating, "To help me think through my decision, I'd like to present my approach to you and ask for feedback to consider before I finalize my plan." The difference is the first doesn't demonstrate authority in your role. Whereas, the second indicates that the final decision is yours.

Disagreements Are OK

Know that if you're going to ask for feedback, then stop and listen to it, even if you don't like what's being said. Accept the gift you're given, tell them you sincerely appreciate their input and that you'll consider it.

If you do disagree, take a moment and ask questions to understand their point of view. Just as with your team, when you ask questions, you gain more insight into a person's thought process and why their providing the feedback they are.

Grow A Backbone

If your role is clearly defined and there's still overstepping on your authority, you can push back and have a conversation. Remember, we're all human and overstepping will happen. The key is to ensure that you are respectful of the overstepping individual's position and authority.

When pushing back, do so with empathy and with deference to their authority. Be curious, watch your tone and ask questions, as this will help to keep the relationship positive and communication open. Something as simple as saying, "I thought this was a decision delegated to me. It sounds like you would like to make this decision. Did I get that right?" in a tentative manner brings attention to the overstepping, but still defers to the authority of your leader. This politely restates the boundaries of each role, while demonstrating your agreed-upon leadership responsibilities.

Get Out Of The Weeds

When sharing with a senior leader or board, share at a big-picture level of the work you're doing to keep them informed. Think executive summary. Too much information puts your board into overwhelm, which may reduce their confidence in you. Your goal in sharing information with your leader is to support them in being more effective in their role by giving them relevant information only. In other words, share enough relevant information so they can be confident in your decisions, without going into the granular details.

Keep It Positive

Never has "it's not what you say, but how you say it" been more relevant. If everything you say comes from a negative tone, your leader may question your competence, causing fear and worry, allowing them to overstep because they don't believe that you'll be able to achieve a positive outcome. When you provide updates to your leader or board, come prepared and confident in your ability to achieve a positive outcome.

Overstepping leadership happens. The trick is to own your part in creating this situation and in how you can resolve it. You are not powerless or a victim of your overstepping leader. Look at your behaviors that may invite overstepping, then see how you can shift it for more positive interactions. In doing this, you're actually helping to lead your board and your team.

IS IT NO LONGER A FIT AT YOUR COMPANY? HERE'S HOW TO MOVE FORWARD

"It's me! I know it! What's wrong with me? Why can't I make this work?"

Something is off, and you can't put your finger on it.

If you've thought this as a leader before, the honest truth is simply that you may not be a fit at your company, and this is OK. Absolutely nothing is wrong with you; you and your company may just be going in different directions. As a leader in your company, this can be an unsettling realization, but imagine what can happen if you stop fighting to make it work and start accepting that growing together is not your future.

How To Recognize A Wrong Leadership Fit

Having heard "why can't this work?" countless times from my clients who are struggling in their current leadership role, there are some questions you should ask yourself to determine if it is a wrong fit.

- What am I trying to achieve in this role?
- What exactly am I fighting for?
- What am I willing to let go of?
- Does this align with where the rest of the organization wants to go?

- If interviewing with this company today, would I want to work here?

By identifying these, you start to bring clarity to why you're feeling the way you do. Then, you can start moving forward.

Other things that often indicate it could be a fit issue, not a skill or talent issue:

- It's always a hard fight to bring initiatives forward and have effective meetings.

- You're not able to use your strengths in your role any longer.

- There's been a gradual shift in the company over time.

- You're not being challenged to grow, but "encouraged" to fit.

- You are never (or almost never) excited about wins or successes.

- You don't feel like you're contributing or being effective.

- Your confidence and self-esteem are at an all-time low.

If you're nodding your head in agreement here, awesome! You're already seeing that it's not you. Next, it's about how to move forward when you recognize this disconnect.

What To Do When It's A Fit Issue

If you've identified that it is a fit issue, you have options. You can:

- **Suck it up**, buy into where the rest of the company is going and stay (Note: I've never seen this work well).

- **Stay in the fight** with the company and hope this will change (It rarely does).

- **Leave.** You need to move on and stop trying to make it work. Chances are, you and the company have outgrown each other or were never really compatible. Accepting this, you can now grow.

It is absolutely OK to leave, especially if it's a fit issue. If you realize that what you're trying to achieve in your role simply isn't going to happen, determine what realistically is the best outcome you're trying to achieve.

If you find yourself having to convince your leaders/the organization's mindset, you're in a no-win situation. It's a bit harsh, but the illusion you need to let go of is that the company needs you. They don't need you to save them. Rather, there is another organization out there that needs exactly what you offer and where you want to go.

Time and again, in my experience, when a client comes to terms with a fit issue and they leave, they nearly always find a better fit shortly thereafter. Knowing how exactly to leave and keep your confidence intact is a key part to moving forward.

- **Accept.** It's not you, and it's not them. This can improve how you approach coming to work in the time being as it removes the pressure of trying to be someone different. Knowing you're going to leave can remove the fight as you transition away.

- **Identify.** Where do you want to go next? Start networking and taking on a work search. Reach out to headhunters and your personal network, conduct informational interviews with trusted colleagues, mentors and friends to help you get clear on what's next, what values are important to you in an organization and what your "must haves" are in your next role in order to bring your strengths forward.

- **Ask.** Have the hard conversation with your company and ask for a package. This doesn't work all the time, but organizations can partner with you to help you make your way forward. Keep this as positive as possible, such as saying: "I've thought about my role here and realized that we're just not a fit. I hope we can come to an agreement to find a person who is the right fit." Then carry the conversation from there.

Recognizing that you and your company are going in different directions doesn't mean that there's something wrong with you or your leadership skills. You create great value — after all, why would you have been hired/promoted as a leader in the first place? You may just have a different future than what you thought. Remember that your strengths will be a competitive advantage when you're in the right company for you.

Ask yourself what's harder, continuing the fight or finding fulfillment elsewhere?

HOW EXECUTIVES SHOULD BE SPENDING THEIR TIME

As you develop as a leader, you may find yourself taking on more responsibilities while still being involved in the day-to-day or learning how to delegate those tasks to your direct reports. When you become an executive, not only do your responsibilities change, so does the way you spend your time.

Shifting from short-term to long-term.

Executives' scope of work shifts from focusing on the day-to-day to looking at the big picture. Days are not spent checking off tasks, but working on strategic planning and the transition is hard to do. You might be tempted to hold on to some of the daily work but while some roles require leaders to continue delivering work with their teams, in most cases this inability to let go will detract from your efforts spent on strategic work.

Your time should now shift from accomplishing tasks to strategizing and planning. Your task is now to coordinate others, remove roadblocks, advocate and influence—whether it's on behalf of your team, company or industry. You should also be spending time developing and mentoring others.

This begins with building relationships with your direct reports, your boss and even your peers, who could be great sources of support or understanding. Your peers don't need to work at your company, or even within your industry, to understand what you may be going through. These relationships help inform your planning, process review and research, helping you to understand your own industry trends and opportunities.

Leaders know that they need time to make time for the above, but not all actually do. This shift in responsibilities requires a shift in mindset, especially in regards to what "productivity" and "success" actually mean within the context of your role. The act of strategizing can seem ambiguous and amorphous. Your success is no longer measured over hours and days, but rather by weeks, months and years.

The non-sexy stuff takes a long time to yield results, and it can take a long time for your success to feel tangible. When you're in execution mode, it's easy to check off tasks and feel accomplished, like you have something to show for the time you have just spent on a project. Strategy planning time, then, can feel unproductive.

As an executive, your job is not to be productive anymore. Your job is to lead, manage, plan and strategize. Your duty to your team is to facilitate and let go of protecting, pleasing and controlling so they can produce. Trying to take over tasks robs someone else of the opportunity to learn how to do them and take ownership of them in the long term.

Strategy time is productive time.

Do you book strategy time in your calendar but end up rescheduling for other projects that feel like more of a value-add? One of my clients says that these time blocks feel "vulnerable" because you're not actually checking tasks off of your to-do list. If setting aside time for strategy planning seems unproductive, it may help to create structure around your reserved time.

One way to do this is to schedule time blocks with a high-level agenda. Assign yourself tasks within that strategic agenda, such as spending 20 minutes reading articles about leadership or your industry. Try writing or actually drawing on paper, a tablet or whiteboard rather than typing on a computer. This can stimulate critical thinking and help you get into planning mode. Even something as simple as naming a strategic project, such as "Budget," or "Look Back," can help provide structure and avoid the feeling of unproductivity.

Reserve "desk days" or half days that are non-negotiable. If I have to reschedule such a time block, I make it a priority to reschedule no later than the end of the week. I also have a day within the week that is unavailable for meetings. Limit answering emails to specific times during the day. Be ruthless—respond to emails quickly, delegate, delete and schedule as tasks to handle later. Periodically review how you spend your time so you can look at what else you can delegate. If you can't currently delegate the tasks that consistently take away from your strategy time, consider developing someone who can take them off of your plate.

Protecting your time.

Your time is precious, and you have to set firm boundaries so that you can actually do your job. I like using the Eisenhower matrix. It designates tasks into one of four quadrants.

Quadrant 1: Urgent and Important —Tasks that fall within this quadrant should be managed by a leader. If it's important to me and urgent, I need to look at what I can do to manage it, delegating as much as I can without giving up my scope of responsibility.

Quadrant 2: Important but Not Urgent— This quadrant requires focus from leaders. If a task is important and not urgent, it's likely strategic and where I want to be spending more of my time, so I need to schedule and protect time for it.

Quadrant 3: Urgent but Not Important (to you)— These are tasks that leaders should avoid. If it's important to someone else and urgent, I should look at what I can do to minimize my personal involvement but make sure the person executing it feels supported.

Quadrant 4: Not Urgent and Not Important— Leaders should limit time spent on these tasks. If it's not urgent and not important to me, I can dump it but I also need to realize that I may be doing this task because I'm feeling burned out from too much firefighting and not enough strategic time.

Besides making time for strategy planning, the most important block in your calendar is time that's only for you. We all need empty thinking space, whether that means going on a motorcycle ride, a solo cross country skiing, a walk or even taking a shower. It feels frivolous, selfish and non-productive, but it's necessary for your well-being as a leader.

IF THERE'S NEVER ENOUGH TIME, TIME MANAGEMENT ISN'T YOUR REAL PROBLEM

We've all been there – scrambling to check the "to-dos" off our list, but finding that 24 hours in a day just isn't enough. "My time just isn't my own," is commonplace in my office as clients describe how they're being pulled in multiple directions and never completing their "top priorities."

Stressed, anxious, and frustrated – burned out leaders want to take back their time but aren't sure where to start. This begs the question: As a leader, how can you start controlling your time when everyone wants it?

Is it your time...or your choice?

First things first, be truthful about whether it's a time management issue or a choice management one.

Answer this: If given more than 24 hours in a day, would you complete the tasks you already have, or add more to your list? Ultimately, it's about making the choices in how you spend your time that allow you to control it.

Once you determine that your choices are the issue, you need to know where you're spending your time. For one week, track all your professional and personal activities and determine:

- Which were proactive or reactive tasks?

- Were they an effective use of your time? (Remember: Being efficient does not equate to being effective!)

- Could a task be delegated?

- Did your proactive leader tasks (strategizing, critical thinking) take priority?

- Were you engaged in all tasks?

- How many times did you say "yes" and wish you said "no?"

By answering these, you'll see how your choices impact whether you are effective or just task checking. The hard truth is that we are often the cause of our own lack of time because of our choices.

Strategize your choices.

Once you recognize where your time goes, you can start making choices based on your goals, values, and priorities. A great tool I use with clients is the Eisenhower Decision Matrix, made popular through Stephen Covey's Time Management Matrix. Using this matrix, you sort your tasks into four quadrants:

- **Do**: Important and urgent tasks. Such things include crisis management, deadlines, and solving problems.

- **Decide**: Important, but not urgent tasks. Examples include planning and critical thinking strategies, relationship building, and recreation.

- **Delegate**: Urgent, but not important tasks in relation to your responsibilities such as interruptions, activities, meetings.

- **Delete**: Unimportant and not urgent tasks, considered time wasters.

By understanding where your choices fall on this matrix, you can start to make decisions based on priorities in the Do and Decide quadrants, specifically by:

1. Delegating tasks.

Make decisions that support your priorities and schedule time for these. If there is a task on your list that does not support your priorities, delegate it. If you can't delegate a specific task, look at the gap as to why not. For instance, do you need to develop a team member prior to handing off these tasks?

2. Understanding your boundaries.

Recognize what your critical priorities are and set boundaries around them. For example, you may need strategic thinking time, but can't schedule it because you're running between back-to-back meetings. By zeroing in on what your priorities are, you're better able to assess which meetings are in line with your priorities, decline those that aren't, and then schedule strategic thinking time into your now open time slot.

3. Setting expectations.

Set expectations and give yourself permission to share them. Here, you must look at your priorities in relation to your goals and make decisions around them. To do this well, you must be honest with what your true priorities are. This will resolve a lot of the inner conflict as to whether or not you need to be doing something over another task.

An example of this is my client who had guilt over not being with her family because of her responsibilities as CEO of a prominent marketing company. When she determined her family priorities, such as attending the majority of her son's basketball games, she partnered with her executive assistant and built her schedule around saying "no" to certain items that fell on game times wherever possible. She allowed herself the freedom to be engaged at his games along with releasing any guilt about being there because she consciously determined which choice was her top priority at that moment.

The biggest shift for my clients when they go from a "time" mindset to a "choice" one is that they end up with free time. They now have space to use for proactive thinking or choosing how to fill this open time in relation to their priorities. In addition, many:

- Let go of outside guilt

- Have less anxiety around free time

- Become engaged and refreshed in conversations and tasks

- Feel they have choice in controlling their time

- Are empowered to make changes in what to say "yes" and "no" to

While you can't control time, you can control your choices and priorities. It can be difficult at first, but by being accountable with your choice management, you give yourself permission to say "no" to things that don't support your priorities. Choice is about spending your time and energy on what's important. And while you can't have it all, you can have the things that matter most to you. Ask yourself: Is it really a time issue…or a choice one?

IT TAKES COURAGE FOR LEADERS TO END THINGS WHEN NECESSARY

A client of mine told me he was reading the book *Necessary Endings* by Dr. Henry Cloud. The title of the book struck a chord with me. The phrase "necessary endings" was provocative and yet intuitively made sense. Most things come to a natural end, but this is still a concept we all struggle with at times and often avoid.

Whether it's a business relationship, a contract, a job or even a standard operating procedure, things can and will come to an end. However, the responsibility to recognize and initiate an ending can fall upon senior leaders and executives—and it takes courage to move forward from an ending because of the discomfort change brings.

The Necessary Endings Leaders Are Faced With

When we think of necessary endings, the most relatable example for many is likely around dating. You might be seeing a person who, despite your positive romantic feelings for them, you don't see a future with. It may not be either party's fault, but hurting them is the last thing that you want to do, so you might delay having "the talk."

At work, these necessary endings can be big decisions with massive implications, or they could be relatively small. Some examples of endings at work include relational situations like letting go of an employee that isn't the right fit for your team. An executive may decide to leave an organization because they've outgrown it or the business has gone in a direction that isn't right for them anymore.

Other endings might be around business outcomes. You may need to end projects that you had high hopes for but are no longer connected to the strategic direction of the organization or aren't producing the desired results. It may involve closing a failing business or wrapping up product lines that are unprofitable. It could even be doing away with services or products that suck the life out of your team members who deliver them.

Endings could also come in the form of transforming how you and your team work. You may change organizational structures that are creating confusion. You may scrap processes that are no longer effective for the current stage of the organization. You might decide to stop having meetings that provide little value, like status update meetings where everyone takes their turn but there is no discussion. It could even be as simple as giving yourself permission to cut down your own workload, saying "no" to a list of 30 strategic priorities to say "yes" to your top one to three.

Deciding When Something Has Come To An End

Even when we start to recognize that something needs to end, we delay decisions and hope that time will reveal the path forward. It takes tremendous courage for a leader to assess a situation and recognize that they need to initiate an ending and make some tough decisions. There are three Es that you can check to help:

- Emotions. Pay attention to your frustration levels, feelings of helplessness, dread, avoidance, overwhelm or heaviness.

- Energy. How much time, energy, resources and attention is something taking? Is it costing too much? Are you spread too thin, sacrificing greatly to ensure resources for the good? Do you have a lack of energy around something that used to create great energy?

- Excuses. Are you or your team making comments like, "That's just the way he/she/it is," "What are we to do?" or "We have to just accept it for what it is."?

Once you've checked the above, you need to decide if an ending needs to be made. If an employee is not working out, what can you do as their manager to support them? Or do you just need to let them go? It takes courage to make the decision and to deal with the "now what?"

I once worked for a company that had signed a contract to get a custom program designed for internal use. I remember the many difficulties that employees were having with the project and much of the feedback was shared with management during the process. It was a classic example of the sunk cost fallacy—there had been too much time, effort and money put into the project not to see it through. But it didn't change the fact that the software didn't work for the company's needs. It took years of frustration, time, effort and more cost before the leadership team decided to finally scrap the contract.

Things might not work out and that's OK. The psychologist Carol Dweck says that failure is necessary. But there is a difference between taking failure personally and admitting when you've made a mistake and moving forward.

I worked with another client who had a sales leader who was toxic to the rest of the organization. The leadership team was scared of the fallout of letting go of this person because of their seniority, legacy knowledge and established external relationships. There were a lot of "what ifs," so it took them several months to finally let go of the employee. However, within 30 days, the sales team performed so well that they surpassed what they had achieved with their former sales leader. Truthfully, when you have a "toxic" employee, they're probably not happy with their current situation either. In this case, the leadership team needed to be able to trust that they would not only weather the loss of an employee, but that they could achieve success without them.

Avoiding an ending, especially when the ending is difficult, keeps you stuck in an uncomfortable position. When we hold on to the difficult, we also hold ourselves, our teams and our organizations back from growing. Leadership requires stepping into tough situations where you might experience loss or pushback. Every ending brings about change, big or small. Will it be difficult? Yes. But you need to lead your team through that change.

ACCOUNTABILITY

Accountability is the glue that ties commitment to the result.

~ Bob Proctor

A ccountability cannot be given; it can only be taken. It's a mindset, a way of thinking, a choice.

Have you experienced circular commitments from a team member or found yourself worrying that, without your presence or constant checking in, things won't get done? You can't truly hold anyone accountable – they have to make that decision for themselves – but you can create an environment where people *choose* to take accountability.

Accountability starts with you modelling accountability as a leader: building strong and trusting relationships with your team, following through on your commitments, empowering others, and embracing learning from mistakes, including your own.

It's not easy to create these conditions. It requires feedback, tough conversations, getting really clear on what you're asking others to commit to. Accountability also means giving people autonomy with guidelines over rules and policies, and allowing them to fail to show you that they can and will follow-through, perhaps even go above and beyond.

And, when they struggle, allow them to struggle and provide support through coaching, challenging, and guiding.

ACCOUNTABILITY AND THE ROLES
WE ALL PLAY

In leadership, accountability is often used interchangeably with re-sponsibility, but they are not quite the same. You can give someone responsibility, but they have to *choose* to be accountable—you can't compel someone to do it. Accountability is about going the extra mile, but it's up to the assignee to step up and to follow through. You can delegate tasks, but not accountability. When you are an accountable leader, you recognize that we all play a part, and you think consciously about the part that you play.

In the workplace, our responsibilities are usually covered by our job description. But even in teams where roles are well defined, account-ability is important because it is shared, and it goes beyond our own tasks. Your accountability, or lack thereof, ultimately determines how you succeed together as a team.

When I facilitate workshops and talk about accountability, I like to show a video from Lead India called "The Tree," which opens with a large uprooted tree that has fallen in the middle of a busy road. People are stuck in gridlock, complaining about why they are stopped and airing their frustration. On the side of the road, people are yelling at each other to do something about the tree, but then comes a down-pour. In the midst of the chaos, a young schoolboy approaches the tree and tries to push it out of the road. Other young children see and join in his effort. Finally, a group of adults comes in, and together, they all move the tree out of the way. The young boy did not need to take action, but he did. He stepped up and played a part.

Holding Your Team Members Accountable

As a leader, it is your job to hold your team members accountable, but accountability must be clear from the beginning. Establish clear expectations upfront if you're asking for commitments from your team members.

For example, when you walk into a drugstore, you might first encounter the person behind the beauty counter. They may ask if you're looking for anything specific. If you are, they may tell you where to find it or lead you right to it and perhaps even ask if there's anything else that they can help you with. Or, they may not even ask you in the first place and just let you shop on your own. If the overall goal of the store is to make sales, leadership should set expectations that they want to focus on the overall customer experience in the drugstore, and everyone is expected to assist customers as they encounter them. This way, everyone—from the associates working the beauty counter to the electronics department—is accountable.

However, conversations around accountability must come from a place of curiosity and learning in order to be effective, and not come from a place of naming and blaming. If a customer didn't find what they were looking for and they weren't offered help, instead of asking why, ask what happened. Effective leaders emphasize shared responsibility with each other: "What happened? What was your part? What did you think was my part?"

As a leader, talk with your team about accountability and what the team's expectations are. If they expect you as a leader to hold everyone accountable, I recommend discussing the importance of the team engaging in accountability conversations with each other and establishing a shared responsibility for those conversations.

Holding Yourself Accountable As A Leader

Accountable leaders play active roles. Delegating goes two ways: You should provide support to see a task through, but you also can't micromanage. Continually ask yourself, "What is my part?" When giving feedback, explore what role you played in the situation, even if it was a small one. As the saying goes, "If you are not part of the solution, you are a part of the problem."

Accountability is contagious. The more you demonstrate personal accountability, the easier you make it for others to step up and demonstrate their own accountability. Accountable leaders walk the talk and model the behavior they want to see. It requires vulnerability and courage to own your part. When you show others that it's OK to own your part, they feel that they can do the same, and they respect you more for doing so.

The Ripple Effect Of Accountability

When there's no accountability, we feel stuck, and sometimes, leadership can play a role in that. I recall when I was a member of a particular professional organization, there were a few members who complained about things all the time and suggested great ideas they wanted the organization to implement.

One day, the leadership team shifted their approach. They started saying to members, "That's a great idea, and you seem to have a passion and vision for this. Would you be willing to volunteer to lead it and see to its implementation?" Some stepped up and implemented the change they had been asking for, while others stopped complaining because they didn't want to own their part of seeing it through. It turned out that some members just wanted the opportunity to step up. When leaders changed their mindset and removed the barrier to ownership of the projects, these members accepted the invitation to contribute.

When everyone is accountable, there is more optimism and hope. This leads to changes in culture with greater trust, collaboration and healthy conflict that allows everyone to dig in and solve issues. This, in turn, increases productivity and performance. People don't hold grudges or let their frustrations drive their behaviors. Instead, they have more tough conversations and speak up before issues become really big. Teams create greater innovation when everyone looks for their part in creating solutions.

The most important part of accountability is that leaders speak up early and often and not wait for someone else to do so. Someone needs to go first, and for a leader, doing so creates opportunities for everyone to do their part.

WHAT TO DO WHEN GETTING
CIRCULAR COMMITMENTS FROM YOUR TEAM

There's nothing wrong with being skeptical of the overly optimistic "Yes!" from a team member when you've asked them for a commitment. You've had the same conversation and the same response before, but for some reason, your expectations weren't met. You're wondering if maybe, just maybe, this time will be different; the yes will be followed by real commitment, and action will finally happen.

While yes and the optimistic "Everything is under control" are great to hear, your gut is telling you that nothing will change. And you know your gut is right.

So, why are you having this same conversation with the same results again and again? More importantly, how can you turn this conversation into a productive and effective use of time?

Reasons For Circular Commitments

There are many reasons why this could be happening. From the work I've done with executives and senior leaders, the most common tend to be:

- Your people are too optimistic about their time and/or abilities.
- Your initial expectations were not clear.
- Your team is avoiding hard news or other issues.

- You didn't receive a real commitment in the first place.

- Your team is afraid to disappoint you.

How To Get Real Commitment

Whatever the reason you're having the same conversation with empty accountability again, it's crucial to take action to stop the cycle and move forward.

1. Own Your Part

Begin by looking inward and noticing what your part is in these conversations. For instance, are you modeling behavior that discourages people from saying no to you, either directly or indirectly? Do you follow through and own your mistakes? Were you clear on your expectations and your reasons behind them? Is everyone working with the same definition of commitment? Are you fully engaged in conversation by listening fully, outlining clear boundaries and allowing them to ask questions? How have you responded to hard news in the past: positively or negatively?

By looking at yourself and identifying how you could have communicated differently, you give yourself a place to begin changing the conversation.

2. Get Clear Commitment

When you're ready to stop the merry-go-round, have a conversation with your team about commitment and boundaries. This will ensure you are all operating from the same rules of engagement. Together, you can agree:

- That saying no is an option in order for a yes to be a real yes.

- How to negotiate when a no has been given.

- How to work together by asking the specific requirements of each individual.

- What your obligations to each other are.

- How to communicate if things go off course.

By defining these, you create a safe environment for your team to pro-actively ask questions and share information with you, even if it's not an answer that you are keen on hearing.

3. Let Your Team Be

Stay out of things until your team has missed their commitment. If they didn't "blow it," and you feel the urge to check up on them, you may need to adjust your expectations for next time if you realized you required something more.

4. Look To Learn, Not To Blame

If a commitment is missed, seek to learn rather than to place blame. For example, ask, "What happened?" rather than "Why isn't this done?" for missed deadlines. This form of questioning gets people to tell you the story rather than getting defensive or telling you what you want to hear. "What happened?" can lead to a more truthful answer, allowing you to then guide them to a commitment with, "What do you need to do now to make this right? Are there any hard things I need to hear? How can we move forward?"

Give them the opportunity to learn and hold themselves accountable.

5. Discover Through A Debrief

If a commitment is missed, there must be a conversation about differ-ent steps going forward. Guide your team with, "What are you going to do differently this time?" but also provide them the opportunity to let you know what you can do differently as well. A hard truth is that sometimes people not telling you the whole story could be how you're getting in the way. Allow them to tell you so, in the respectful manner set out in your rules of engagement.

The bigger focus to remember is that cyclical conversations in which you're always being told what you want to hear come down to trust, commitment and accountability. If you're unable to build trust and obtain a real commitment, how can your team be held accountable?

It's better to hear a hard truth and be able to act than to not hear it and have to deal with the aftermath from any fallout. By allowing people to provide you with an accurate commitment based on your jointly defined rules and expectations, you remove doubt in your gut, build trust in your people and move forward with real confidence.

How are you going to turn your conversations into real, actionable accountability and commitment?

POLICIES VS. GUIDELINES: HOW TO SET CLEAR EXPECTATIONS

Company culture is largely influenced by senior leaders, which is why continuously working on your leadership skills is critical. Corporate policies are equally impactful on company culture. Having worked in HR, I have seen both great examples of corporate policy and clear ways of how *not* to enact and enforce company policies.

Yes, Policies Are Necessary

If you read stories about companies (particularly fast-growing start-ups) having bad or even toxic company culture, it often comes from a lack of policy or guidelines. Some organizations do not have policies at all, which results in employees not being aware of the expectations of them within their work. All employees need some form of guidance in writing as a foundation to understand their roles. Guidelines also help people understand the values-driven behaviors of the organization. In tough situations, they can look to these guidelines and act in alignment with the organization's values.

When To Put Policies Into Place

While all organizations should have policies of some sort in writing, it is especially important when they hit growth milestones. This is when you start to have multiple managers, teams, departments, branches or divisions, meaning more room for interpretation and misinterpretation of expectations. Early corporate policies should document procedures, such as who does what, or deal with customer issues, such as refund policies. This helps create consistency throughout an organization as it grows, especially as you begin to lose the ability to have everyone report directly to the C-suite. Without policies in writing, your employees would spend a lot of time trying to figure out how things are supposed to be done as opposed to actually doing them.

There are definitely instances in which having clear corporate policies is necessary for everyday operations, no matter the organizational growth stage. This includes policies to ensure employee safety, such as work-alone policies or even anti-harassment policies. There should also be policies that would grant the company more authority in gray areas, covering instances that may not occur often but that staff will still need to be prepared for (i.e., potential crises). Should the situation arise, employees will know what they need to do.

Beware Of Corporate Policy As A Rule Book

Many organizations can be too heavy on corporate policies: They have too many and are too detailed. The policies become policing items, as opposed to guidelines to establish consistency throughout the organization. The problem with such policies is, first and foremost, that no one will read them—even other leaders within the company. I have even seen companies with thick binders full of policies that write out actual legislation in full, which could render these policies out of date if legislation is changed or updated, when simply pointing to the legislation would suffice.

Some companies write complicated policies that can be overbearing and sound condescending. The employees meant to abide by the policies may even feel scared, because they feel like they do not know or understand the policies at all, and that they would have to keep referring to the documents because they are bound to them. For example, a customer policy that forces someone to treat every customer the same when there are differing circumstances for customers doesn't allow for the employee to do the "right thing," only follow the rules. As a result, they may feel that they lack integrity and lose motivation to do a great job because they are afraid to stray from the strict outline that dictates their actions. They may even feel vulnerable to being reprimanded. Ultimately, policing people lowers morale and damages company culture.

How Policies Should Be Written Instead

While there are times where a hard policy is important, leaders often convince themselves that everything must be perfect and allow for no variance to get the best outcomes. This is not accurate.

Areas such as employee safety, compliance, conduct and employee leave will always need clear rules. Outside of these specific areas, corporate policies should be concise and instead offer guidance to employees. From there, you should have conversations with your employees to set expectations and boundaries. When talking about boundaries, Brené Brown suggests a structure using "what's okay and what's not okay." Instead of trying to come up with policies that cover every actuality, companies should allow for critical thinking and judgment. If an employee is not meeting the expectations set for them, you have the opportunity to find solutions and accommodations, given their circumstances, and set them up for success in the future.

Anywhere that you'd like to leave your team members with the ability to interpret and use critical thinking to apply the expectations to their unique environment may be a fit for expectations conversations in lieu of formal policies. For example, many companies are using a dress code policy that simply says "Dress for your day" and leave it to the team member to use their judgment, good or bad, to dress appropriately for their work.

When drafting policies, think about the core issue that you need to actually address. For example, some companies have instituted policies against using business phones for personal calls or using the company computer for personal internet use. Then came smartphone bans. The core issue was never the second screen but that the employees were not doing their jobs because they were distracted. Identifying the core issue allows you to address it and set expectations accordingly.

Good Policies Empower Employees

Know the difference between your nonnegotiables and areas or actions that can be left to your employees' best judgment. Opening up critical thinking at the employee level creates a culture of consistent decision making throughout the organization. Policies, when used effectively, empower employees because they feel like they are backed by the company and that they are given the authority to exercise good judgment. Good policies give employees a background for consistency and authority at their job and guide them to act in accordance with organizational values.

NOT GETTING THE RESULTS YOU WANT FROM YOUR TEAM? IT COULD BE YOU

It's Monday morning and you ask Laura, a member of your team, to develop a slide presentation on your company's best business practices, saying it's due Friday. What you forget to mention is that you'll be presenting the slides first thing Saturday morning to your company's board of directors.

All week long, you see Laura working away on her computer, not really interacting with other members of the team, and never sending a draft of the presentation for your initial review. When 4:30 p.m. on Friday rolls around, you're still (anxiously) waiting for the presentation from your team member. You finally hear the *bing* in your email, breathing a sigh of relief to see the presentation in your inbox.

However, when you open the slides, they are on the wrong practices you wanted to speak to the board members about, leaving you to pick up the pieces and develop the presentation yourself. Clearly, Laura failed.

Or did she really?

First, acknowledge the step you took as a leader by delegating the slides to Laura. Unfortunately, you were let down. Yes, there are things Laura could have done to make sure the presentation was what you wanted. But, how could you have handled the above situation differently, whether in the moment or prior to assigning the project? How could you have ensured that your expectations were clear so Laura could reach out for help if needed and be more committed to completing the project before 4:30 on Friday?

Harsh as it may sound, chances are if your team is letting you down, you're letting them down in some way. The good news is — you're part of the solution!

Clarity In Delegating

As a leader, it's crucial to delegate to your team to allow you to focus on your strategic planning responsibilities. However, when you delegate, ask if you are being clear on your expectations.

For instance, with the above example, you could have indicated:

- The slides should cover company practices X, Y, and Z.

- The audience is company board members.

- The purpose is to understand company culture.

- The presentation time is 9:00 a.m., Saturday morning.

- The draft must be in by Wednesday at 2:00 p.m.

- The final version is due Friday at noon.

This clarity provides a better understanding of why the presentation is being developed, who it is for and what parameters are required for success. There are also accountabilities set with deadlines and purpose, which allows the opportunity to "fail" on a first draft in order to grow in developing skills and creative thinking on the next version.

By providing clarity, you support your team's likelihood of achieving the results you want.

It also invites your team to ask questions to remove any confusion and build stronger conversations as you support them in their own growth.

Relationships On Your Team

Do you know what your team's relationships with each other are like? Will your team support, collaborate and mentor one another, while still holding each other accountable? If yes, then you are empowering them to think about the bigger picture, using their individual skills to work together to achieve a positive result. In doing this, you build your trust in their abilities.

Had Laura been in this type of environment, she may have:

- Reached out for more clarity.

- Asked for support in reviewing the slides before sending to you.

- Been more committed and engaged in creating the slides.

- Built your confidence in her skill set for further growth.

If you don't have this type of team environment, then it's time to start having some crucial, often uncomfortable conversations to build a higher-functioning team. In these conversations, you learn how to best hold your team — and yourself — accountable to results. You give opportunities for your team to voice their concerns or questions, along with identifying where you may need to tweak your communication style and what will engage your people on a project.

Relationships With Your Team

Just as your team needs to build relationships between themselves, you must do the same with them. In getting to know your people beyond the task at hand, you start to build a partnership with your team, encouraging more discussions over dictations. You start to understand what their individual values are, what motivates them individually and what will engage them in their projects.

Let your people own how they do their work, so long as it's in line with your organization's values. Your responsibility is connecting them to the why behind the work, tying them to their purpose on the project, and what the parameters for success are.

For instance, perhaps Laura is excellent at building visually beautiful presentations as she values creativity. Had you connected to this value of hers, indicating why this is important for the presentation to be successful, along with providing clarity around the project's parameters, she would have been more committed and engaged in the success of the project.

Ultimately, to start getting the results you want, it comes down to having better conversations where everyone is clear on expectations. In using this type of approach, you're helping to develop critical thinking in your people, along with asking for a commitment in a way that resonates with them.

Remember, at the end of the day, everybody wants to create results and do a good job. The question is how can you get there in a way that everybody is growing, engaged and committed.

HOW TO COACH AN 'UNCOACHABLE' EMPLOYEE

Many leaders who have worked their way into a senior position have had some tough experiences managing employees along the way. Whether the employee is underperforming or exhibiting problematic behavior, the situation can be stressful for all parties involved.

However, saying an employee is "uncoachable" is a serious conclusion. Leaders should first look to themselves to recognize the real issue at hand and see if there are solutions to be found for that issue.

Uncoachable Versus Ineffective Coaching

If you are having trouble working with your direct report, you must first ask whether you are labeling someone too quickly as "uncoachable." Sometimes, the issue is not that the employee is uncoachable, but rather the leader doesn't know how to coach. You're directing, controlling or convincing, instead of asking questions and being curious about what's happening for your team member. What have you asked of the employee up to this point? Have you been clear about their performance? Do they know, without a doubt, what your expectations are? Have you told them that you are frustrated?

It is important at this point to do a self-check. Are you asking questions? Or, are you simply telling (and calling it "coaching")? Avoid just telling them what to do or convincing them of your point of view, and instead, look at the areas you might need to improve.

Understanding What Motivates Your Employee

Your employee might not be responding to your coaching because they are driven by different motivators than the goals and motivators you've set for your team, and they are unable to admit that to you. They might also simply be feeling stuck. The key is to initiate conversations to learn about what your employees want and what motivates them — and ultimately, create an environment where they feel safe to share this with you.

In his book *Drive: The Surprising Truth About What Motivates Us*, Daniel Pink posits that human motivation is intrinsic and that it may fall into one of autonomy, learning or purpose. A deep understanding of what motivates your employee will unlock a new perspective from which to provide feedback and might transform your interactions.

What You Can Do Early On

Use feedback to test if someone is coachable. Talk about your relationship and feelings, not just tasks, by asking about your employee's story or experience. Be sure to separate facts from your own interpretation and feelings. Create a checklist that allows you to assess how ready you are to give feedback. (I trained with Brené Brown's organization and find her engaged feedback checklist to be a helpful example of this.) If you can't say, "Yes," to everything on your list, you're not ready to give feedback.

You can also use the situation, behavior and impact model—a strategy for addressing behaviors in a way that also describes the impact of those actions—to give feedback and ask a lot of questions.

Stop only talking about the work, and start building a trusting relationship with your employee. Get to know your team members, and have regular one-on-one meetings. Ask for feedback on how you can become a better leader to support them in their growth. And when giving feedback, offer it as information for the employee to consider what they want to do with it. If needed, give them a few days to think about it, and then they can come back and discuss what their next steps should be. If they don't accept the feedback, don't force it on them. Rather, set clear expectations and boundaries, and ask them what support they need to meet those expectations. It's key to build trust with your team.

I've found helping your team bond with one another can also build trust. Some tools, such as personality assessments, can encourage these connections. Consider implementing programs that open up vulnerable conversations as well. One example is Patrick Lencioni's activities to build connection in the team by sharing your most significant achievement and why it is important to you. In my experience using this tool, participants often share personal stories, which can help groups of people get to know one another. It can also create safety for the "uncoachable" team member to start experiencing trust in the team by sharing their own vulnerable story and having the team listen.

When An Employee Is Truly Uncoachable

To be uncoachable means that someone's mind is set and they are unwilling to change. I can't coach someone to run a marathon if they don't want to run. I first have to coach them to find their motivation on *why* they want to run. If we can't find that, we're done.

An employee might be uncoachable if you repeatedly provide feedback and they ignore the issues. They might exhibit passive-aggressive behavior, focus on being right or blame others, and they could be overly controlling of their own and others' work. I've found this is often a fear response that is linked to the fear of not being good enough. They can't see that their behavior is negatively impacting their efforts to get to where they want most.

If you feel like you are approaching this point, it is important to document the entire experience. Involve human resources in your discussions with your employee. Don't let their negative behavior go on forever. Do everything you can to test if the person can be coached, and then move on when necessary. Time doesn't make things better — only action does.

As a leader, keep working on your ability to give effective feedback. Ask curious questions. Assume employees are doing the very best they can (even if they're missing the mark), and practice being vulnerable in relationships with employees by sharing your thoughts and feelings, not just facts. As a leader, it's your responsibility to have greater accountability in the relationship, so look inward and assess your own coaching skills so you can coach others in a way that they will be motivated to respond.

TIRED OF BEING "MONKEY IN THE MIDDLE"? HOW TO HELP YOUR TEAM WIN THEIR OWN BATTLES

Your door is open, you encourage people to come to you with any issues and you've been a supportive leader. But now? You're the go-between for your team as they complain and whine about other team members, fighting their fights and winning their battles for them. Nothing gets accomplished (although your step counter is up for the day), and you feel exhausted from listening to issues without hearing any solutions.

Stop being the monkey in the middle as their go-between and become a leader who empowers your team through coaching. The above type of three-way relationship is reflective of the "drama triangle," a common phenomenon in workplace relationships that often sees leaders unable to find or create long-lasting and empowering solutions. Rather, this back and forth creates more damage and less engaged employees.

Dropping The Drama

What's crucial to create empowered individuals is removing the drama from the drama triangle. Yes, it's that obvious. And this triangular relationship isn't just between individuals. It's also at play within companies where the drama happens between different departments. Regardless of individual or department, it's possible to move towards a positive outcome once you've identified that you're in the triangle.

Stop And Own Your Role

"I'm just trying to help."

"They need me."

"They can't solve it without me."

"I told them I would."

If any of these rings a little too true, ask yourself why. Chances are these thoughts are enabling the drama. Recognize what actions you're taking that contribute to the triangle and how you can start to create a different outcome.

Start Asking Questions

Ask each individual involved what they hope to get out of this situation along with what they could do to get it. By having them find their own solutions rather than you trying to solve them, you support them in finding an outcome they're comfortable with. Not sure where to start? Ask them to:

- Recognize their part in the scenario

- State what outcome they want

- Identify what they are willing to do to create what they want

Set Reasonable Boundaries

Let people know what boundaries you are setting and then stick to them. Examples of what this can look like are:

- "It's OK to come and talk to me, but it's not OK to come and vent without then finding a solution."

- "I can coach you on how to approach Peter about this issue, John. However, I will not go and talk to him on your behalf."

- "I will be a mediator at your and John's meeting, but I will not have separate meetings about it afterward."

- "Tell me how I can help you help yourself."

Yes, people may be disappointed in you for not saving them, but know that this is OK. This can be one of the hardest parts of leadership. Ultimately, by not jumping in, safety floaties and all, you're now supporting them in finding an impactful long-term solution or relationship rather than a short-term Band-Aid. Your role as facilitator is purely to enable people to come together to identify an agreed-upon way forward. This is your opportunity to take on the role of coach and not rescuer.

Enabling Empowerment

As you practice coaching rather than rescuing, the following skills will support you in creating engaged critical thinkers:

- **Neutrality:** You must remain a neutral party at all times, even if you agree with one party.

- **Empathy:** Demonstrate empathy to allow each individual to feel heard and validated while staying neutral. For example, say, "I'm sorry you're dealing with this," not, "I agree, this isn't right."

- **Active listening:** Be engaged in the conversation, even if you're there as a fly on the wall.

- **Open-ended questions:** Make the questions you ask open-ended, as this helps to engage people in their critical thinking. For instance, ask each person to tell *you* what they need rather than having you tell them what they need.

- **Self awareness:** Notice, as a leader, when you play the role of victim and how you model this behavior to others. This will help you discover how to coach yourself in owning your part and recognizing what your options forward are. The best way to minimize the power of the drama triangle is to model the behavior you want reflected. Want a team of critical thinkers who are empowered to work through their issues in a respectful manner? Then you need to start reflecting this by no longer being the rescuer of your team, but the leader who coaches them to find their own solutions.

The truth is that any time there are more than two people, there will always be potential for a drama triangle. The good news? You have the power to remove the drama simply by owning your part, then helping others own theirs to move forward. This is your power as a leader.

TOUGH CONVERSATIONS AND HOW BEST TO APPROACH THEM

As leaders move up in their careers, they are more likely to have tough conversations with people within and outside of their organization. Tough conversations are necessary in all roles in order to progress through difficult situations. While we have all put off tough conversations or avoided them altogether, great leaders must know how to approach these conversations and face them head on and make sure to consider the other party when they do so.

Why We Avoid Tough Conversations

People put off tough conversations because they worry about the outcome: what might happen during and after the conversation. We want to be able to control where the conversation goes.

There are three kinds of tough conversations: giving feedback, sharing a tough decision or trying to influence the other person to come to a decision in your favor. The last kind is particularly difficult because you have a vested interest in the outcome.

Every time you step into a difficult conversation, vulnerability plays a role. Vulnerability is uncertainty, risk and emotional exposure. This is precisely what makes conversations difficult: the unknown outcomes, the feeling of emotional exposure, and not knowing how the other person will respond. This is what causes people to delay having those conversations and giving feedback.

Initiating A Tough Conversation

So, how must a leader approach a tough conversation? First, you must ensure that you are ready to engage in the conversation, feedback or otherwise. Brené Brown has an Engaged Feedback Checklist which lets you self-assess if you are ready to have this kind of talk.

The next and most important step is to ask for permission. This means that "no" must be an option for the other party as well. In the book *Beyond Reason: Using Emotions as You Negotiate*, Daniel Shapiro and Roger Fisher listed five "core concerns" for every negotiation or tough conversation:

- Appreciation

- Autonomy

- Affiliation

- Status

- Role

These five concerns ensure that the other party feels safe in a tough conversation. By asking for permission, the other person may feel that their core concerns are acknowledged. If a conversation must happen, give the other person the timeframe and ask them to come see you when they are ready.

Lastly, be clear on the type of conversation that you are about to have. Are you giving feedback or sharing a decision? Sometimes, we call it feedback when it's really not.

Also, is it an influencing conversation where you want a specific decision from the other person, and you might be disappointed if they don't agree? Sometimes you just don't come to an agreement, but you must find a solution and move the conversation forward in some way.

Knowing the answers to these questions should help you get in the right frame of mind for this talk.

Key Aspects Of A Tough Conversation

Some people say that emotions have no part in business. However, in tough conversations, emotions will inevitably play a role. A great leader listens not just for content, but also for emotions.

Be ready to handle the emotions that arise. If tears come up, don't pretend that they are not there. Emotions inform us during conversations about what is and isn't OK. Sometimes, it shows us that it's OK to walk away from the conversation when we need to, to take some space so we can pick it up again later. You might need to have a series of conversations instead of trying to push for a result in a single discussion. Know when it's necessary to apologize.

Open up the discussion by choosing your words carefully and with empathy, seeking to understand the other person: "Help me understand ..." "Tell me more ..." "What's important about ..." You must also recognize when your own safety or the other party's safety is at risk. Remember the core concerns listed above.

Tips For Specific Conversations

As business leaders, you may face tough conversations regularly with specific groups of people.

If you need to have a tough conversation with a direct report, a colleague or an employee within your organization, consider what you want for them, not what you want the outcome to be for you. Be aware of who has the power, and recognize the environment you are in. If someone is not your direct report, the power may rely on their leader, not on you.

Tough conversations with a leader or a client are put off even more often. You might feel more at risk with them because they convey the power in the relationship. In this case, it is paramount to speak tentatively, keeping safety and respect top of mind. Rather than asserting truths or facts, opt for statements such as, "I was wondering why …" "In my opinion …" "I'm beginning to wonder if ..."

Lastly, here are some tips for any tough conversation:

- Speak from the heart and a place of vulnerability.

- Separate sharing facts from interpretations, assumptions or impacts.

- Use feeling words and "I" language to express yourself, and consider your tone of voice and body language.

- Be direct with empathy. Brené Brown says, "Clear is kind, unclear is unkind."

- When you make a mistake, own your part and reset the issue, or stop yourself and explain that it didn't come out as you would have liked and try again.

- Use the Situation-Behavior-Impact (SBI) format for giving feedback. Show without shame or blame.

- Practice! We tend to build it up in our minds that we have to wait for something really big to have a conversation. Practice talking about small things before they become big things. Then, when something bigger or more uncomfortable comes up, you will have had plenty of practice and it will be easier, even if it is still uncomfortable.

- Consult references such as *Crucial Conversations: Tools for Talking When Stakes Are High*, *Fierce Conversations: Achieving Success at Work and in Life One Conversation at a Time* and *Dare to Lead: Brave Work. Tough Conversations.*

Tough conversations aren't always easy, but I hope that the above tips inspire you to face them head on, with courage and vulnerability.

HOW TO LEAD THROUGH
BIG (AND SMALL) CHANGES

C hange is difficult for everyone. In business, some changes are so monumental that there is an entire profession dedicated to it: change management. Change managers are specifically brought in usually in times of organizational change, such as mergers and acquisitions. However, there are some changes that leaders need to manage on their own and help their teams get through the transition period.

In simplest terms, change management is helping people through the process of change when we are hardwired to prefer the status quo. As human beings, we are not always good with change, and changes in the workplace are no different.

Companies usually bring in change managers when there are external factors. But sometimes, even for big organizational changes such as new executive leadership or restructuring, change managers are not brought in and the process has to be managed internally by leaders already within the organization. If you are a leader, you are likely to manage changes for your team at some point.

Thinking Of Change Management As Change Leadership

While a significant amount of planning can go into managing the organizational changes that affect the financial, organizational and process structures of an organization, it is also important to manage the effect of the changes on people's emotions. This is where change leadership comes in. Leaders need to coach and lead their teams through the transition period—helping people to accept change, holding them accountable and reminding them why the change is happening and what's waiting for them on the other side. Change can bring about significant emotions. Not only do you have to address your employees' concerns, you also have to allow them to grieve the loss of comfort and what is familiar.

The Kübler-Ross Change Curve is an often-used model that shows the emotions that people go through in times of change. In this model, the first stage is shock. This is common especially for people who did not want the change. Over time, shock becomes denial, and then there is a period of frustration and then depression. Eventually, a person will start to entertain the idea of change and experiment with that change before going into decision mode and ultimately integration.

Even people who encounter change that they want experience a similar curve. In place of shock, they may have a short honeymoon period during which morale increases. However, as they navigate the change and perhaps start to see some gaps between expectations and reality, they may have an even steeper fall into frustration and depression before being able to go into experimentation, decision and integration. Change is difficult because it often requires a change in ourselves.

Coaching Through Change

In this period of frustration and anxiety, it is crucial for leaders to step in and help people move through the change curve; people can get caught up in the drama triangle, where there is a struggle between victim (the person), persecutor (the change) and seeking a rescuer.

Do not forget that you might have also gone through your own curve when you learned of the changes that you are now navigating your team through. Leaders have to face their own challenges with the change while supporting others, creating alignment with their team and supporting momentum when things get hard.

The leader is generally ahead of their team in the change curve process and that can leave their team feeling disconnected from them and create a credibility gap. As a leader, you will need to use empathy skills to reflect your desire to understand others' emotions and where people are in the curve. The X-axis of the Kübler-Ross Change Curve is labeled "time," but what that time looks like can differ for each person and each circumstance.

Change Leadership And Communication

Leaders need to be able to communicate the importance of a change to their team. You might even be able to plant seeds about an upcoming change. Part of the difficulty with change is that people do not see that there is a problem that needs to be solved, necessitating change. Clear communication of change must answer these three questions:

- What? (What is the change in the simplest terms? This is something that you may need to reiterate as you move through the change process.)

- So what? (What does it mean for me?)

- Now what? (What can I expect will happen next?)

Leaders can help their team members move through change-inspired frustration and anxiety into courage, even if it is with baby steps. Leaders can challenge teams and ask, "What's your part in this? Given the circumstances, what do you want out of this?" Most importantly, leaders need to empower employees throughout this time. What is the purpose of the change? What might they be losing sight of? People need support through change and to be reminded of the good things that are waiting for them on the other side.

Anticipating Change

Changes, big or small, can trigger the emotional rollercoaster that is the change curve. It's only natural for people to wonder what is going to be different for them. What's going to happen with my role, how others perceive me and how I work with others?

Leaders should anticipate what they need to do when change comes, and not just for big changes. Make sure to show empathy and appreciation of effort. Acknowledge your team and recognize how far they have come. Ask them what they need to get to the next step. Create alignment with your team, and support momentum when things get hard. Do the work to move through change together.

RECHARGE

Rest time is not waste time. It is economy to gather fresh strength ...
It is wisdom to take occasional furlough. In the long run,
we shall do more by sometimes doing less.

~ Charles Spurgeon

At the start of coaching, many of my clients were members of one of three clubs:

1. Can't get to sleep club
2. Awake at 2 am for two hours club
3. Up at 4 am club.

They didn't suffer from traditional insomnia, but what I called "spinning mind". They couldn't turn their thinking off because they had nowhere else in their day to think.

It's impossible to have innovative, strategic, or systems thinking when you're on constant overdrive. If you want to have space for thinking, you must create that space. I've had clients who do their best thinking on a motorcycle ride in the country, or cross-country skiing alone, or when they keep up with a regimen of reading fantasy books before bedtime. Our brains need a break from thinking all the time.

The constant dopamine hits of checking off your to-do list feel great short term, yet at the end of the day, can leave you feeling drained with your brain still craving thinking soak time. Serotonin is what sustains long-term thinking and energy to regulate your sleep, mood, and digestion. Low levels of serotonin lead to greater anxiety, depression, pain, and aggression. Want to sleep better at night? Want to drop the 20 pounds you've accumulated because of stress at work? Want to be more composed and resilient as a leader? It all starts with creating space and rituals for rest and recharge, including exercise, getting outdoors, and eating well.

A recharge looks different for every leader; uninterrupted holidays, a sabbatical, an untouchable day of the week, or regular habits like reading, exercising, and more. What is consistent is the personal commitment to rest and boundaries.

UNLOCK THE BENEFITS OF TAKING A WORK BREAK

A lot of leaders, unfortunately, have one thing in common: the inability to take a break. Whether it's short breaks away from the desk or computer throughout the day or taking advantage of accrued vacation days or paid time off, leaders pack their schedules with back-to-back meetings with no time to eat or even think in between. I've often booked coaching sessions where we order in for lunch because clients in leadership positions weren't able to take a lunch break.

There are a number of signs (apart from all that built-up vacation time) that you need to take a break. You may struggle to think clearly and have feelings of being foggy-headed and confused or you might experience analysis paralysis. You may find yourself focusing only on the negative and becoming overwhelmed, as if nothing will get better. You may feel overcome with emotion that seems disproportionate to a particular event and even have mounting conflicts with colleagues, friends or family.

Take a rest to build resilience.

Taking a break doesn't just mean stopping what you're doing and working on something else. It means having something to eat, going for a walk or actually resting—giving your body rest and reprieve along with something that it needs.

Our minds and bodies need breaks in order to function at our best—that's backed by science. A Scientific American article stresses the importance of downtime as it "replenishes the brain's stores of attention and motivation, [and] encourages productivity and creativity." This downtime allows our brains to process recent events, a practice that in turn helps us develop our sense of self, as well as improve how we relate to others.

I often speak with my clients about building resilience. Resilience isn't only about bouncing back, but about coming in with a full gas tank. You have to start from a positive position to be able to return to a positive position. When you rest, you become a rubber ball and are able to bounce back. When you ignore your needs, you become a glass ball that can crack or shatter under pressure.

Breaks can be as small as taking a regular beverage and a restroom break, having a meal or getting outside. When you don't take breaks you can get mired in challenges and, in turn, may lack the mental energy to take a wider view. Challenges look different when you step away from them, but it's difficult to take a wider view without actually getting mental or physical distance.

Enjoy the immediate benefits of breaks.

When we take breaks, even small ones throughout the workday, the benefits we reap can be immediate in both clearer, longer-term thinking and in shorter-term, strategic systems thinking.

Leaders might feel like they can't think straight or make decisions but experience a-ha moments in the shower or on a walk or bike ride or even on the weekend—"it made sense all of a sudden" or "it just came to me"—but it's actually because they were finally able to take a break.

We also need a variety of interests and pursuits in life, and balancing work interests with our other interests—mental, physical, vocational and spiritual—is key to our well-being. Pursuing these interests stimulates our brains and exercises them in ways that are likely different from how we use them at work.

We do our best work when we let our thoughts marinate for a while and then come back to them. That's why some people do their best thinking while in the shower, walking the dog, going for a run or painting.

Vacation time is not just a perk.

Vacations don't have to mean going on holiday or a trip to a faraway destination. You can use your vacation time to nourish your well-being without going anywhere, but it's important to spend your time off like you are away. Be unreachable. Treat yourself to sleeping in, long showers, long walks and a lot of rest.

Set yourself up with the kind of food that makes you happy—maybe it's from your childhood or maybe you desire time spent cooking your favorite meals. Some people pick up home improvement projects or pursue passions like competing in a marathon, which can also be fulfilling. Vacations are key times to do things that bring you renewed energy.

For some, completely unplugging might be unrealistic, so they may want to do some work to keep up, but it's important to set boundaries on how much work you let in. Ask yourself: How much are you really needed? How much do you trust others to keep working while you take time off?

Not taking breaks is a real issue with senior leaders because the pace of the role is intense. Unfortunately, I have worked with some people in the past who have ignored warning signs and have then had to take mental health leave in order to recuperate.

That's why it's important to review any of your own built-up vacation time. One of my clients had several weeks of banked vacation time on top of their annual vacation allocation, and we worked together to enable and empower him to actually start taking that time off. Vacation days are not just part of your compensation package—they exist to ensure you are taking care of your well-being.

Take your breaks by choice.

It's easy to come up with excuses for why we're unable to take breaks. There's a lot going on, and before you know it, you've missed lunch, you haven't gotten up from your desk in hours or you've maxed out your accumulated vacation time.

We need to mindfully make time for breaks. Put your lunch break in your calendar so you don't get booked for meetings. Set an alarm so you can go for a walk. Even better, plan all your vacation days ahead of time and set them up for the whole year. Breaks allow us to replenish our mental energy, and in turn, our physical selves, which allows us to be at our best, not just at work, but in all aspects of our lives.

LEADERS ARE ALLOWED TO SLEEP TOO: HOW TO STOP SUFFERING THROUGH SLEEPLESS NIGHTS

"*If I could just get some sleep...*"

A simple, yet common statement I hear from C-suite executives, higher level managers, and others in leadership roles when we first start working together. In fact, more than 80% of leaders I work with indicate that their critical and strategic thinking, along with responsive abilities, are impaired because they are exhausted. Meaning, the results they want to create aren't being realized.

What does this mean for them as a leader? Think of it this way: Just as driving while tired is likened to driving while drunk, showing up to work exhausted is like showing up to work intoxicated, which can impede your ability to develop the strategic work that you, as a leader of your company, have to complete.

I say this to raise an awareness of what a lack of sleep can have on leaders. With this awareness, you now have a choice as to what you can do to resolve poor sleep patterns. So, how do you know if you're suffering from sleepless nights?

Your Mind Goes On Nightly Runs

Your mind is never as active as it is when you're trying to sleep. This is a primary symptom that my clients highlight as their first indicator of lack of sleep, not the physical ailments. This typically shows up in three ways:

- Not being able to get to sleep

- Waking up in the middle of the night, including popping in and out of sleep

- Waking up really early and not being able to get back to sleep

With this sleep pattern, my clients identify that their minds are:

- Sorting through ideas from the work day, or starting on problem-solving

- Reliving conversations that happened during the day and are now trying to work through them

- Beginning to think critically because they haven't carved out critical thinking time during the day

Cognitive Effects From Lack Of Sleep

There is a plethora of research on the effects that a lack of sleep can have on your body and overall physical health (e.g., weight gain, cardiovascular risks, depression, etc.). However, it's just as important to understand the effects it has on your mental capacity, namely:

- **Reactive vs. Proactive Thinking:** Always being reactive to situations and putting out fires rather than building and implementing strategic initiatives for your company, can lead to higher levels of anxiety.

- **Reduced Team Engagement:** You may have lower levels of empathy for team members. This hinders your ability to coach them – a common requirement for leaders – because your emotions are maxed out. Part of being a leader means being able to effectively support your team when they need you. When you're exhausted, you simply don't have the emotional capacity to deal with others in a way that moves conversations forward.

- **Tunnel Vision:** Sometimes tunnel vision is a great thing, keeping you focused on a specific goal or target. However, tunnel vision due to lack of sleep often impairs your ability to have an open mind for critical thinking—meaning, you may be closed off to beneficial business solutions.

Start Combating A Lack Of Sleep

"Just get a good night's sleep" is not a solution. After all, when my clients are dealing with prolonged sleepless nights, it becomes about building the proper tools for effective sleeping patterns rather than a quick fix. Here are three ways to get started:

1. **Build and benefit from a support structure.** As leaders, we tend to think that we have to have all the answers and handle all situations on our own. Really, the opposite is true. It's important to surround ourselves with individuals who can support us, whether that is at the office, managing the day-to-day activities of the business, or externally, such as having a coach (an objective third party) or peers that you can trust and share your challenges and successes with. Above all else, I have witnessed first hand that this is key for leaders to start effectively sleeping.

2. **Get ideas out of your head ASAP.** There is nothing wrong with having ideas pop into your head when you're relaxing. By letting your body relax, you're giving your brain permission to do so, which is when it will provide solutions. However, the trick is to get the idea out of your head so you can quiet your mind. How? Put a

notepad on your bedstand. If you wake up with a thought, write it down. This way, you'll remember the thought without having to worry about forgetting it. This helps you clear your mind, allowing you to release the thought and go back to sleep.

3. **Create healthy habit strategies.** Looking after your physical and mental health are crucial for good sleep. Be sure you eat—and eat well —exercise, develop healthy personal boundaries, both in and outside of the office, and give yourself downtime to recharge. Try journaling to get what's on your mind down on paper and out of your head, and proactively carve out non-negotiable critical thinking time during the work day.

If you, as a leader, are finding that sleep is an issue, then I encourage you to look inward at your own habits and support system. In doing this, you'll proactively identify why you're not sleeping and develop solutions accordingly, setting yourself up to be a more effective leader with greater impact on your company.

HOW TO BALANCE WORK AND PERSONAL OBLIGATIONS OVER THE HOLIDAYS (AND YEAR-ROUND)

It's the most wonderful time of the year. When balancing work and family over the holidays is discussed, most advice seems to center around completely unplugging from work. However, this isn't always feasible for senior leaders and executives who cannot completely disconnect because they play essential roles or are required to at least be reachable. Some companies can close their offices over the holidays, but in some industries, like manufacturing or retail, it's just not possible.

Regardless of the holiday or time of year, there are ways to strike a healthy balance when taking time off if you can't completely unplug from work.

On the work side:

Set and enforce boundaries with your staff and yourself.

Many leaders can't completely disconnect during the holidays due to the nature of their work or because other demands keep them at least semi-connected. If an extended period of time off isn't feasible in your role, you can give yourself mini disconnect breaks, like meals without electronics. You also can only check for emails or calls periodically for urgent requests. I personally like to set aside 10-minute triage blocks when I have time off. This lets me check my emails but forces me to use the time diligently because I know I only have those 10 minutes to assess what's urgent versus what can wait until my return. The same principle applies to phone calls. These correspondences can easily become a time suck, so setting a strict time limit for yourself can help enforce those boundaries.

The same technology that makes us constantly available also can help us disconnect. Some phones have "do not disturb" features that you can set to require people to call twice before they can get through. This reminds them to think about whether the nature of their call is truly urgent. You can also manage how often emails come through or whether you need to manually fetch them.

Practice what you preach.

In my experience, modeling behaviors of disconnecting (as best as possible) during time off can help you build trust and show integrity as a leader. When you tell your team to disconnect but then practice the opposite, it can come off as a silent form of judgment. They might think, "My boss doesn't think I'm promotable because I'm not working hard enough." They'll likely feel not only that your words and actions don't align, but also that it's not actually okay for them to follow your advice.

Talk about expectations before you leave. I'm not a fan of policies, but I am a fan of talking about norms—what you can expect from each other and what each person on the team needs during the break. You hired grown-ups, so let them be grown-ups and manage themselves.

If your team tries to contact you during your time out of the office, you may respond with, "What's most urgent at this time?" or "This doesn't sound urgent; maybe this can wait until we're back in the office." Sometimes, it's better to just say no. The other person might be disappointed, but they'll likely support your decision.

Plan for a realistic and balanced share of responsibilities.

Responsibilities don't always have to be specific to one person. Meet with your peers to set expectations and figure out what you need from each other over the break. Can you set an on-call schedule for the team so everyone gets some relief while out of the office? Can you appoint a first point of contact who can manage requests for different leaders? Executives must also decide what's imperative for business continuity. Maybe your finance department can take time off, but you need IT personnel on call. The impact on each company is unique, so it's important to assess this ahead of time.

Your executive assistant is your strategic partner. Work with them to manage your workload, perhaps in the lead-up to your time off or when you come back. Lean on them to help manage your emails, phone calls, meetings and so on.

On the personal side:

Set expectations and boundaries with family and friends.

Talk to your family and friends about expectations and the support you might need from them at this time. If your role requires you to be connected in some way, set aside some nonnegotiable time frames where you could work if you deem it necessary. If work demands your attention, ask your family for permission to address any issues that are pulling you away, and ask that you won't be made to feel guilty about doing so.

On the flip side, ask your friends, family or partner to hold you accountable. If you promised to only check emails for 15 minutes each day, honor your promise.

Lower your expectations, and don't overbook yourself during your time off.

The pressure to do it all is real, but you can greatly reduce anxiety and more effectively recharge during your time off if you don't expect to do everything at once. If you normally host a big holiday dinner, see whether someone else in the family or friend group can either tag team it with you or take over this year. If you're going away on vacation, make sure you have some time between arriving home and getting back to work. As much as we all want to maximize the time we have, it's also important to be able to scale down your plans to the essentials so you can guarantee protected time for yourself and your loved ones.

At this time of year, and anytime you take time off, remember that what's urgent and what's important aren't always the same. Ask yourself: What's more important right now—spending time with family or closing a deal? On the other hand, should you be attending parties or responding to critical incidents? Effective leaders set boundaries and priorities to help them answer those questions and achieve balance.

HEADED BACK TO WORK AFTER A BREAK? HERE'S HOW TO NAVIGATE THE CHANGE WITH RESILIENCE

The journey to senior leadership can be filled with change. Sometimes we move into new roles by way of promotion or entrepreneurship. But for many others, we may have found ourselves starting a new job or re-entering the workforce after a break: a layoff, a sabbatical, parental or medical leave, a merger and acquisition or simply because we quit a job without having another one to move on to. Although the circumstances can be different, the emotions brought about by these changes are often the same—and leaders hardly talk about them.

What To Do When You've Just Left Your Job

Whether you have chosen to leave your role temporarily or permanently, have been laid off or need to take medical leave, you are now faced with a significant change in the way that you spend your time and energy. For a lot of people, especially in leadership positions, it can be difficult to switch off. We might feel pressure to "keep up" professionally during this time.

Whatever the reasons, the most important thing to do with this time is to take a break. Be intentional about regrouping and reflecting. If you are on parental leave, take the time to focus on your growing family. On sabbatical? Concentrate on your studies or travels. If you've had to take medical or stress leave, then you definitely need to take the time and space to get better. I know of a company that would actually cut off the emails of a person on medical or stress leave so they wouldn't feel tempted to check in. If you've just been laid off or quit your job, figure out your next steps. This is not something that everyone is able to do, but if you are, use this time to think about what you want next. You may feel ready to return once you've actually taken a break.

Filling Your Cup During A Break

The time after leaving a job may be particularly emotional. That's why it's important to give yourself permission to take a break so that you can come back with a full gas tank and have energy to propel yourself through. Spend this time on yourself. Hang out with family and friends, try yoga or meditation, journaling and exercising. Engage in regular learning or develop a new skill.

You don't have to work on your professional self at this time. Fill your time with non-work activities. Find new hobbies or volunteer for the sake of creating an impact, not just to add to your resume.

When you are ready to put yourself back into work mode, you can work on your leadership skills again. Engage in industry events, take a course, read leadership books and listen to podcasts. Just don't fill your time only with professional development; your personal development is equally important. Embrace your life right now, especially the things that you enjoy, without guilt.

The Emotion That Comes With Going Back To Work

Once you do return to work, whether coming back from leave or starting a new role, there can be intense conflicting emotions: excitement over a new start, but also a sense of loss for the life you may have led while you were away from work. Your feelings might range from confidence and acceptance, to anxiety, overwhelm, vulnerability and trepidation—sometimes all at the same time. These emotions are all valid, although you may also feel guilt for the negative emotions that come up. You are not alone in feeling this way. Tap into your inner circle to help process how you feel.

Adjusting To The Challenges Of Being Back At Work

No matter how long you have been away, if you're coming back to an old role or starting anew, you should assume that everything is different. Ways of working have evolved. Relationships will need to be reformed. You might feel a little rusty. Impostor syndrome may kick in at this time.

If you're feeling unsure about your leadership skills, tap into the resources at your organization. Adopting a growth mindset instead of a fixed mindset is especially important when starting a new leadership role. Take a listening tour. Do informational interviews with each of your peers and team members but also with other leaders across the organization. I would recommend seeking mentors above and below you to help you learn new policies, processes, technologies and updates in your industry.

It's also important to take the approach outlined in Michael Watkins' book *The First 90 Days* and resist the urge to make immediate contributions. Watkins' book is specifically intended for leaders who are starting new roles. If you are a senior leader, you may face some anticipation around your arrival from the organization. Take time to learn about the new role and be transparent about what they should expect from you, especially in the early days of your new job.

This strategy can also be applied when returning to an old job. If you're coming back to a role, people may expect you to jump back in right away or for things to go back to how they were. Intentionally put the brakes on and manage the expectations of your team.

Navigating Changes With Resilience

Something that I constantly work on with my clients is the idea of building resilience. The period of transition in between roles is a particularly important time to build that resilience. In fact, your resilience will definitely be tested during this time.

This is a shared experience for leaders that needs to be addressed. We need to normalize actually taking a break and not feel the pressure to work on ourselves professionally all of the time. We also need to normalize the conflicting emotions that come up when leaving that break and going back to work. The less pressure we put on ourselves to embrace this time, the better it will be for our personal development.

LEADERSHIP TEAM

Great teams do not hold back with one another. They are unafraid to air their dirty laundry. They admit their mistakes, their weaknesses, and their concerns without fear of reprisal.

~ Patrick Lencioni

Every leader has a team. In fact, leaders often have more than one team, including the team of their peers, the team of their direct reports, and many others. What you may overlook is the importance of your team of leadership peers and making your relationship and work with them your number one priority.

To be effective, your leadership team must be cohesive, aligned, and behave as one leader of the organization. This begins with shifting your mindset to see your peers as your number one team, not your direct reports.

Building relationships with your peers beyond doing the work is essential to directing an organization as a true leadership team. It takes work to reach alignment, and alignment doesn't always mean agreement. It takes consistent communication to maintain a cohesive leadership approach while keeping your own unique leadership style. This communication includes building deep trust, getting clear on values and expectations; it can even take the form of a formal or information leadership team manifesto.

To truly break down silos in an organization, start with developing effectiveness within your leadership team.

THE POWER OF BUILDING
A LEADERSHIP TEAM MANIFESTO

Have you been going through the motions as a leadership team, feeling siloed and more like bland vanilla pudding than leaders who boldly grow and inspire your organization? Even if you can't describe it, you know that you could all be better as a leadership group.

In working with leadership teams that feel this disconnect, I often start by focusing on who they are as a team and what their collective manifesto is. Even if leaders want the same things for their company and teams, they may not have an agreed-upon commitment in how they'll get there together. They do not have a team manifesto for their own leadership group.

What is a manifesto, and why is it important?

A team manifesto is a document that highlights:

- Behaviors that embody your shared team values and purpose

- How you work together

- What you do and do not stand for

- How you hold each other accountable to remain a united front

While we often think of manifestos being for front-line teams, it's important for leadership teams to have one, as it acts as a compass so you know you're all going in the same direction. Your manifesto is a commitment to one another, defining what you're moving toward together and giving you permission to hold each other accountable along the way.

When you have a defined manifesto that your team believes in, you're able to:

- Make consistent decisions

- Bring more cohesiveness to relationships between one another

- Trust each other to respectfully challenge, debate and persist through obstacles

How do we develop a team manifesto?

No worthwhile team manifesto ever came from sitting in a boardroom and asking, "What do we stand for?" Manifestos only have power when people believe in and connect with them. Developing a team manifesto is about connecting your shared stories and values together to define who you are as a team.

Sit down with your leadership team and talk about what stands out from your shared experiences. As you do, note where similarities exist to help identify:

- What's important to the group

- Who you want to be together

- Commonalities in your personal values that help to build your team

What can a manifesto be?

There's no right way to develop a manifesto. What's important is that it holds real meaning for your people — otherwise, it will be yet another writing exercise that sits in a desk drawer.

I will say that the most effective manifestos I've witnessed in action are those built around who the team was. Here are a few basics to help give you an idea of what a manifesto could be for you:

It can be any length. I've seen manifestos that are one sentence, ten lines or even a few paragraphs.

It's okay to be playful and bold and to include metaphors. A colleague's client has a manifesto that includes, "Tell it like you're six beers deep." Doesn't mean much to anyone outside of the team, but to them, it's a reminder of their team-building event where one of their most reserved members had a few beers and finally opened up in a way that was positive for their team and company. Thus, "six beers deep" means something to them — it's memorable and likely to create a greater commitment to the manifesto.

Simplicity is okay. Grandiose, life-changing affirmations are fine, but your team manifesto doesn't have to have them. Something as simple as, "We're all human and deserve respect" is sometimes all that's needed.

Acknowledge your bad habits, but account for how you're improving them. If your team has bad habits, such as speaking down to one another, they won't disappear just because you say, "We speak respectfully to one another." Acknowledge that you may still speak disrespectfully, but note how you hold each other accountable when this happens. For example, "We sincerely apologize when we disrespect each other." Eventually, the bad habit will work itself out, but it's won't happen overnight.

It can be aspirational. You may not be the leadership team you want to be now, but by creating an aspirational manifesto, you're developing the commitment — and the accountability — required to become one.

It doesn't need to be understood outside your team. It's for your team only and it should mean something to them. It shouldn't be watered down with pretty marketing language that speaks to everyone, as it will lose its meaning and depth for your team. One leadership team's manifesto includes, "We tell each other when we have poppy seeds in our teeth." To them, it's a commitment to have each other's backs, no matter how bizarre or uncomfortable.

It should be updated. Your team manifesto today may not work for the team you have in a year. If your team is disconnected from the manifesto, revisit your shared experiences and values as you are now and see if the manifesto needs to be reworked.

The only way right way to develop your manifesto is to make sure it has real impact and meaning to connect with your leadership team's shared experiences.

If your leadership team is missing a commitment to each other for how to lead, go back to your stories and build your manifesto. And what if you don't have any stories? Perhaps it's time to get away from the office and get to know who you are as a leadership team.

HOW TEAM COACHING CAN HELP YOUR EXECUTIVE TEAM LEAD AS ONE

As an executive coach, I have worked with hundreds of individual senior leaders over the last several years. Coaching executive teams can be quite similar to individual coaching in a lot of ways—especially if you view your team as a singular leading entity.

Teams are made up of individuals and yet a team's impact is greater than the sum of the individual's contributions. Team members have an interdependent relationship with one another to achieve common goals, tasks and a company vision. Team coaching helps the team see this interdependence and the strengths, obstacles and potential of the team when it works in harmony to find its own answers. In essence, team coaching involves, at its core, systems thinking.

Often senior leadership teams are composed of leaders who head their own departments. An executive team meeting may then feel like a battleground of sorts, where each leader's goal is to represent and fight for their direct and indirect reports—their own team. However, as business author Patrick Lencioni has written in his book *The Five Dysfunctions of a Team*, for the organization to succeed, the leadership team has to be your number one team. The development process of team coaching enhances a leadership team's overall systems thinking beyond their immediate team.

Team Coaching Vs. Team Building

Some might think that team coaching is the same as team building. While team building is important, team coaching is about digging into the tough stuff to create tangible alignment and cohesive teams. Team coaching includes a blend of coaching, teaching, facilitation, mediation and positive psychology. It helps your leadership team lead as a consistent principal of the organization.

Think of your relationship with the leadership team as if it were a marriage. Team building is like going on fun dates together. It's important to have fun and regular alone time as a couple, but it isn't enough if the couple focuses only on having fun and avoids having conversations about their goals, their future and where they might fail to find alignment. Team coaching is where you step into the "work" part of the marriage. But if a couple only ever does the hard work and never has any time set aside for activities together, they can grow tired of always doing "hard work" and this too can erode the relationship. We need time to both be in the relationship and work on the relationship.

Individual Executive Coaching Vs. Team Coaching

Executive coaching is important to help individuals work on their mindset and development as a singular leader. Team coaching works with the whole "team" at once—not the individuals—to develop as one cohesive system. We coach the system itself and the relationship of the team. Both are important aspects to bring a leadership team to peak effectiveness.

Team coaching looks at the interactions between individuals in a way that can't happen in one-to-one coaching. When working with one leader, we can dig in deeply on helping them develop their personal skills and leadership effectiveness. But, when one person changes, the whole system must change and adapt. Sometimes this change is difficult, even if it is desired by the rest of the team or organization. We can do great work with one individual who can have an unintended positive or negative impact on the relationships within the team or the whole organization as a result. No one is an island. When one person changes their behaviors, they change the norms of the relationships. Others must adapt to the new way of being in that relationship and working with that person.

Executive coaching helps a leader become more effective in their role. Team coaching helps each role become more effective within the team. However, a team member can move between roles and the system still needs to be effective. Teams rely on roles to complete their unique functions and tasks. Empowered team members share the load and lean on the team for solutions rather than have all the answers. Team coaching ensures the group has a healthy ability to generate those solutions and execute on them.

Just like executive coaching, there are elements within team coaching that help a team be effective, such as relationship goals, team assessments, team leadership and 360 assessments, identifying team purpose, creating a vision for the team and understanding what the team is collectively yearning for.

Team coaching helps teams work together with deeper trust so they can engage in healthy conflict and debate and get behind the group decisions, even if they would not make those decisions themselves. They find greater organizational clarity and the ability to communicate consistently with others in the organization as a whole. While business workflow and decisions may remain difficult, teams develop a process to work through conflict, rather than getting stuck in it.

Who Needs Team Coaching

Team coaching can help teams work through decisions where there are no right answers. The process can help strengthen trust with one another and increase alignment and accountability. It can be valuable to any executive team, but teams that are experiencing some issues can benefit the most. These could be teams wanting to level up their collective leadership and become a more aligned, less siloed leadership team. They could also be leading the organization through change or currently experiencing persistent conflict or challenges with one another or experiencing a sense of feeling stuck. There may be teams struggling with any level of team dysfunction from mild to toxic, or on the contrary, teams that don't engage in conflict and are stuck in false harmony, meaning everyone is nice but no one is candid with one another.

Team coaching isn't a one-and-done experience, but a developmental process just like executive coaching. The team must commit to regularly working together on their relationship and the system as a team and maintain the behaviors they've developed through the process.

THE OPPORTUNITY YOUR EXECUTIVE LEADERSHIP TEAM COULD BE MISSING

As an executive leader, your primary team shouldn't be the one you are leading. This is a bold statement, yes, but hear me out. Your primary team for ensuring results must be the executive leadership team to which you belong.

Without an executive team collectively leading, a company may be successful, but not sustainable. I'm not saying that all leaders must have the same leadership style. Rather, the executive team should be aligned on where they currently are, where they want to go and how their teams will cohesively work together. This creates long-term, sustainable success.

Executive team coaching can help bring alignment to the vision of where a company is going and how each leader on the team plays a role. In fact, executive coaching isn't necessarily about transforming poor leadership teams into great ones, as even great leadership teams may inadvertently fail to lead together despite their successes. It's about breaking down the silos between teams, starting with the leaders.

For leaders, it's important to understand the reality of your leadership team's effectiveness. By looking at the truth, and not your individual perceptions, you'll be better able to answer what's keeping you from being a cohesive team. Even if you are achieving great results today, as a team, you should still ask if the leadership team is creating a longer-term tornado.

This takes a level of vulnerability but helps create a culture of learning, inviting leaders to remove the fear of looking at the reality of individual effectiveness. You are now able to have candid and safe discussions on how to be even more effective by leading together.

Assess For Strengths And Gaps

To begin understanding how coaching can bring alignment to your executive team, you must first do an evaluation of where the team is currently at. This can be done either through conversations with each other or through an objective tool that highlights both strengths and gap areas, such as a 360 development assessment tool.

Through this honest assessment, you understand what your strengths are (what you're doing well) and where there could be opportunities to grow and become better, and you identify what skill sets or talent gaps might be missing on the leadership level based on where you want to go. This puts into context where your leadership team (and therefore, the company) is starting from, so you gain better clarity on everyone's role in moving toward your vision.

Identify Your Start And End Points

Through this phase, you develop what your commitments are to each other, which will help the leadership team identify:

- Why the team exists in the first place—your purpose

- Who you want to be as a team, centered on values and behaviors

- Where you're starting from as a team in relation to where you want to go

- What strategy you execute together as a leadership team as well as your strategies for your individual teams

- How you will relate to each other

Essentially, what you identify becomes your road map for where you want to go. It's a big *you are here* starting point.

Design Your Route

Once coaching helps identify where you are, who you want to be and where you're going, you then design the "how." These are the various routes or tactics you can employ to achieve your strategy. These routes will include:

- **Relationships:** How do you build relationships that sustain through challenges? What do your trust, communication, cohesion and synergy look like?

- **Goals:** What structures, processes and behaviors must the leadership team have in place to ensure alignment for achieving a goal?

- **Responsibilities:** Is there clarity what your roles are, what accountability looks like and how you'll work together to achieve the defined goals?

- **Performance Management:** Have you developed a method to assess your effectiveness as a leadership team —how you know you're progressing, where you're at in your process, etc.?

With an agreed-upon route highlighted, you can move forward knowing your role in moving the company from point A to B on the map.

Aligned Executive Leadership

Through this coaching method, you're able to focus on the bigger picture and understand the interactions between the teams. This allows everyone to recognize what resources need to go where and why.

As a result, a company with cohesive leadership should have multiple touch points for accountability and coaching throughout the year. This allows your executive team to identify if you need to change your route (strategy), but in a way that builds collaboration across the organization. Coaching becomes a development process for having executives work together to have more impact as a company.

Because each executive team is as different as the individual leaders it's made up of, executive coaching isn't really a simple 3-step model. There will be different gaps, strengths, starting points, goals and so forth. The one thing that is constant is the willingness to have honest and candid conversations to stop going through the motions. At the end of the day, executive teams who receive coaching together have real development, both personally and collectively, built around deeper conversations and vulnerability.

Has your executive leadership team come together to see if you're cohesively leading?

DON'T TRUST YOUR TEAM?
HERE'S HOW TO START

Trust. Such a simple word, but not so simple an action, especially when it comes to your team.

Yes, it's important that you create an environment where your team members trust each other and yourself, but what happens when you don't trust your team?

As a leader, it's crucial that you trust your team in order to be effective and produce results. So, when I hear "I don't trust my team" from clients, there are typically three reasons:

- **Leader versus expert issues:** This happens when you have been an expert in a specific area that your team member is now the expert in. This often raises internal issues of whether or not you can trust them to be as "good" an expert as you are. You don't trust the individual's competency, leaving you to want to step in and be the "expert" again, not the leader you are now.

- **You're not the expert:** If you're not the expert in a specific area, how can you trust an individual as to whether they're doing a good job and making the right decisions? This comes from not knowing how to trust your team based on their expertise and whether or not they are making the right choices that fit with your goals.

- **Individual commitment or competencies:** You simply don't trust the individual to be competent in their role because they may not have demonstrated their commitment to the role or team.

Whatever your reason for not trusting your team, the steps to building your trust in them are similar.

1. First, assess why you don't trust them.

Begin by asking yourself *why* you don't trust your team. What's at the core of this lack of trust? For instance, have they broken your trust in the past by not living up to their commitments?

A great tool to use in gaining clarity around why you don't trust your team is Brené Brown's BRAVING Model. Identify if your lack of trust centers around:

- **B**oundaries: Did they overstep your boundaries, knowingly or not?

- **R**eliability: Are they unreliable? Do they do what they say they will?

- **A**ccountability: Do they take accountability for their actions and make amends?

- **V**ault: Have they shared confidential information they weren't supposed to?

- **I**ntegrity: Do they practice their values rather than simply profess them?

- **N**on-judgment: Have they judged in the past or come to interactions with an open mind?

- **G**enerosity: Can you assume that they have done their best or acted with good intentions?

By answering these questions, you'll have a starting point as to why you don't trust individual team members. Once you identify what your core trust issue is, you'll be able to develop a strategy in building trust where you need to.

2. Next, get to know your people.

Have you taken the time to get to know the people on your team? How can you expect to trust them if you don't know what makes them tick?

I'm not asking you to learn intimate, deep, dark secrets, but simply who they are as a person both in and outside of work. This will help you understand them and see them differently, as you'll get to know their values and the benefits that they add to your team. You'll have a better understanding of where their expertise comes from, how they process information, and how they prioritize.

You'll also gain insight around their commitment and competencies within their role on your team. This will inform whether or not they are coachable. You can always teach skills, but you can't teach commitment.

Getting to know the people behind the word "team" will go a long way toward building trust.

3. Finally, focus on trust around values.

Not everyone on your team is going to have the same values as you, and that's OK. What's important is to understand your guiding values *and* theirs. You can then have honest conversations about what's important to you and why, and give them the opportunity to do the same. Depending on the specific project you're working on, if you can directly explain what value needs to be prioritized for a specific task, then your team better knows how to approach the project.

Take the time to identify what you need from your team, such as key metrics and project milestones, then share these with your people. If you don't do this, you're setting your people up to fail because they don't know what you need from them and why.

It's important to note that if you want to trust others, you have to be trustworthy. By modeling this behavior of building trust around values, you don't just build your trust in your people, but their trust in you as well.

Trust will not happen overnight. What's important is to recognize what you own in building trust with your team and not expecting them to build your trust for you. This is like waiting for them to be psychic, which, let's face it, most likely won't happen. Stop waiting for your team to become trustworthy and turn the mirror on yourself. What actions can you take in supporting your team to earn your trust?

SUCCESSION

One of the things we often miss in succession planning is that
it should be gradual and thoughtful, with lots of sharing
of information and knowledge and perspective,
so that it's almost a non-event when it happens.

~ Anne M. Mulcahy

Succession development is such an important concept that over the years, I've given it a project code name to challenge my clients: Project Obsolescence. You can't be promoted until you are no longer needed in your current role; until you have fully developed several potential candidates to succeed you and a solid plan to transition them into your role without business disruption. I know this to be true because I've worked with many leaders who were overlooked for promotions because they were too needed in their current role. I don't want that to happen to you.

One of your most important roles as a leader is to develop those below you to succeed you, and to develop yourself to move ahead and succeed your leader. This is your part in creating organizational sustainability and scalability.

Give and get regular feedback, engage in formal 360 assessments, and create a formalized development plan or road map with a timeline for developing your successors. Ensure you develop more than one successor so they can not only succeed you, but other leaders in the organization. Engage in development that goes beyond business acumen and expertise in your current discipline or business unit and include strategic, systems and critical thinking, relationships, authenticity, self-awareness, cross-functional collaboration, and more that requires exposure across and outside the organization. And succession doesn't begin and end with development, it includes smooth transition into a role. How are you planning for your succession transition and the person succeeding you?

WHY YOU NEED TO MENTOR YOUR EXECUTIVE LEADERS

When it comes to senior leadership roles, most organizations prefer to promote from within due to the risks that can come from an external hire: risks to the corporate culture, risks to the strategic direction, risks in making a "bad fit decision." Just risks abound!

Yet, promoting from within isn't as easy as succession based on seniority rank. It must come from the CEO (or president, or CFO) supporting the development of their senior executives. However, many CEOs I've worked with struggle with mentoring and developing their senior executive team. They feel that their senior leaders already have great depth of business acumen, leadership and strategy, so the fear of "what do I have to teach them?" rings loudly.

The focus shouldn't be on what you have to teach them, but on what happens if they want to become CEO one day (or simply want to take their leadership to the next level, however they define it). What development will they need to undertake to successfully get there?

You are responsible for the growth of your leadership team.

A slew of challenges will arise when you shy away from mentoring your executive leaders. Your attention will be constantly pulled in different directions as your leaders hustle to compete for your time and attention on their quest to further develop. In fact, in Daniel Pink's book, *Drive: The Surprising Truth About What Motivates Us*, he identified mastery as one of the three core human intrinsic drivers (along with purpose and autonomy). Your leaders want to grow and continue improving themselves, just as you do. It is in their DNA. By taking an active role in their growth, even if it's connecting them to the proper individual for mentorship, you ensure they have access to the right resources to reach their next level.

Circling back to the question of "What do I have to teach them?" the truth is you might not have anything to teach them, but that's not what mentorship is about. It's about sharing stories, experiences and challenges that you have worked through. This encourages others to up their game and focus on their development because your experiences demonstrate how to think critically about challenges they will face in the future.

One CEO I worked with identified his discomfort in mentoring his executive team. Through our coaching work together, he also identified this as an area of development he wanted to improve to become a more effective CEO. He noted that avoiding his discomfort was holding his team back from reaching their highest performance because he wasn't connecting to their growth goals. While he saw his executive team as his peers, ultimately, they were also his direct reports. Because of this, combined with his board's top priority of CEO succession planning for the organization's sustainability, he knew he had to face his discomfort to develop succession from within the executive team.

How did he start? It became about informal conversations with his executives, listening to their goals and identifying how he might be able to support their learning.

When this approach is taken, you are able to identify:

- Are there relationships you can help these leaders forge?

- Do they need specific exposure to the board of directors, external stakeholders, customers or industries?

- Are there opportunities you can help them step into, so you and they can predict their future performance in a new role, up to and including CEO?

You should be helping to grow the right soft skills and relationships.

By the time leaders reach these senior executive roles, we assume they have a high degree of technical and strategic competence. Therefore, growth doesn't necessarily need to focus on these aspects. What differentiates leaders at their (and your) levels are the soft skills, emotional intelligence and ability to forge sustainable relationships at all levels within the organization and external to the organization.

Effective CEOs look for ways to facilitate relationships between high-potential executives and the board of directors, look for purposeful strategies to develop enhanced emotional intelligence and leadership skills, and create opportunities for broader business exposure for these individuals. Effective CEOs are also courageous in giving critical feedback with empathy on hard topics for the sake of the executive's learning and development.

By expanding your thinking of "mentoring," you are better equipped to identify the things your leaders need now to grow to where they are going. It becomes about taking a critical and active role in developing succession plans and leaders, not just sending leaders on courses and engaging in executive coaching.

While it may not have occurred to mentor or further develop your executive team because you see them as amazing and competent leaders already, remember, they still need to grow at the executive level, just as you did (and possibly still do). Leading your peers can feel uncomfortable and is often less formal than leading any other team, yet as the CEO, this role is essential for ensuring future leadership of your organization and your own satisfaction in development.

WHY YOU SHOULD DITCH PERFORMANCE REVIEWS (AND WHAT TO DO INSTEAD)

Performance reviews seem to be a given in any workplace. If you are a senior leader or executive, chances are that you have given and received quite a few performance reviews in your career. While a significant part of my job is working with executives as a leadership coach, I am also a certified HR professional in the United States and Canada. Even with my background, I am here to say something that is probably not a popular opinion, especially among HR professionals: Performance reviews don't work, and you should ditch them.

Why We Think Performance Reviews Are Necessary

Performance reviews usually have three goals:

1. Help develop the careers of employees

2. Make decisions on compensation, especially in large organizations, in order to allocate bonuses and raises

3. Figure out whether employees are aligned with business goals and work plans

If you ask me, performance reviews do a terrible job of doing all three, and nobody really knows what to do with performance reviews. Even with my clients who don't actually do performance reviews, employees often ask for them because they want feedback on how they are doing. In the workplace, no news is not always good news. They want to know, "What am I doing well? What am I not doing well, and how can I improve?" Employees want to know where they stand.

At the same time, performance reviews can sometimes hinder the careers of employees. Since they are part of your permanent employee record at your current organization, performance reviews can make employees fearful, especially when they have leaders that they do not get along with. Some employees might even refuse to sign their reviews because they don't agree with them, but in the end, they are still part of your record and can impact your future opportunities within the organization.

Using performance reviews to decide compensation also creates a scenario where a manager must rank employees. Companies typically budget out limited bonuses or raises. If your performance review process involves scoring or rating, chances are, getting four out of five or an "Exceeds Expectations" may make you ineligible for the same score the following year because you already received it before. It becomes arbitrary and quickly loses meaning. No one wants to be ranked as "Satisfactory, Met Expectations or Exceeded Expectations." Often, there are only so many allowed for each ranking and everyone can't get "Exceeded" even if they did actually exceed expectations. This breeds cynicism and it can be demoralizing to become just a number on a scale. I'd argue for giving the same bonus or raise to everyone.

The last reason to conduct performance reviews, on paper, seems promising. Leaders are looking for ways to show senior leadership and demonstrate for themselves that their employees are achieving the organizational objectives and performing well. However, I believe, this should be a separate conversation, not tied to performance reviews.

Why Nobody Likes Doing Performance Reviews

For many organizations, performance reviews land at the same time of year, often toward the end of the year before the holidays or in January. This is right when people are trying to close the company's year-end or get back into the swing of things. It's already a hectic time for everyone.

As a result, performance reviews are often rushed. Leaders struggle to do them because they don't have enough time to thoughtfully prepare and then have all of the meetings. To fit in thoughtful prep time is at least 30 minutes, but typically an hour each, and then can be an hour per employee in meeting time. That's more than a week of work added to everything else going on.

Reviews are also often done annually, which are way too far apart. Trying to assess an employee over a full year is unrealistic. After three months, it can be difficult to accurately remember what happened, and leaders may start filling in gaps with assumptions. If leaders take on the burden of constant documentation, the feedback becomes old and irrelevant.

Employees also do not understand what the expectations are when it comes to filling out their reviews. They tend to write too much, and then leaders get overwhelmed. However, when they do finally get their feedback, they think, "At least I finally know what my boss thinks."

What To Do Instead Of Performance Reviews

The most effective way to actually help develop employees is to give regular feedback year-round. Have more frequent career conversations with your direct reports. Check in with them about their career direction, and their learning and development needs. Create one-page development plans, and be open to changing them along the way. Have shorter, but more regular meetings. Time periods do not have to be finite, but I suggest they be done quarterly at the very least, so that both parties have an accurate memory of how things are going.

Leaders might feel like they need to keep annual performance reviews so they can tick off boxes for HR or the executive team. If you are stuck with the yearly review, have quarterly conversations anyway. Make a few notes each time you meet to complete the standard forms at the end of the year. By then, you can ask, "Does this reflect what we've been talking about?" The "review" then becomes a collaboration between the leader and employee as opposed to something they dread or don't know anything about. I think you will find that it is a worthwhile investment as a leader in the long run, so you can confidently delegate to your team and have better employee engagement.

PASSING THE TORCH: YOUR GUIDE TO SUCCESSION PLANNING AND DEVELOPMENT

As leaders plan their future, they must also look towards a time when they'll step away from leading. Succession planning, as many business leaders know, has a long timeline. But to be most effective, the process must start earlier and have a wider scope than you might think. Senior leaders and executives must always think about succession planning, and be actively preparing for their next step.

Setting Timelines And Building Your Succession Roster

A five-year timeline for succession planning is good, but it's even better to start planning as early as possible. While leaders usually have a date in mind for succession to happen, there are factors that might be more difficult to control.

What if you have to leave earlier than planned? What if the successor you had in mind leaves for another position or even another company? Planning earlier can help you navigate these situations and fully prepare to move on from your role. The last year of your succession plan should be a dedicated transition period for you and your successor.

When people think of succession planning, they might think of a leader choosing a single person to be their heir apparent, who they will groom for the position. In reality, choosing a singular successor poses a significant risk to both the leader and the organization. Rather, leaders must have a short list of candidates in mind as possible successors and work to develop all candidates. Think about the qualities and skill sets that you might want your successor to have. Do you already have specific peers or employees in mind? What if you don't see a clear candidate within your organization? You might even have to look externally to meet your timeline.

Opening Up Leadership Conversations

Once you identify this short list, have conversations with your candidates early on, not only to determine their aptitude but to learn more about them. What are they like as leaders? What are their career aspirations? What level of support do they need to take on this type of job? Would they even want to become an executive one day? Leadership roles can be challenging, and not all people want the challenge or the responsibility. Shortlisting candidates means executives have ample time to learn more about how each candidate operates on a day-to-day basis. Take this opportunity to observe them and consider this in your planning.

Put effort into developing candidates. Because you are identifying them early on, you now have the opportunity to identify any gaps that they may have and give them opportunities to develop their business acumen and the skills required to fill the leadership position. Perhaps at this point they may benefit from further formal education such as MBA programs, or from learning about different functions across the organization, whether that necessitates a lateral move or mentorship from a senior leader within a different department.

To develop their leadership skills, create opportunities either within their current roles or in new roles for them to build skills like systems awareness, critical thinking or even public speaking and presentation skills. This period also gives candidates the chance to identify gaps in their own development and advocate for themselves, so that you can give them the time to work towards closing those gaps.

Succession Planning Throughout An Organization

Succession planning is not just for the C-suite. As senior leaders move into executive positions, they leave positions that also need to be filled, which means they too need to plan for their own succession. Succession planning must occur throughout the organization to ensure the leadership pipeline is filled.

An effective internal succession pipeline means that organizations must provide opportunities for employees at all levels to develop their skill sets. Having leadership conversations at every level is a great start because you'll learn who among your employees are looking to step into a leadership position and you can support their aspirations. As with senior leaders, all levels of staff should be afforded opportunities to build up leadership skills as well as business acumen. Keep lines of communication open and exchange feedback to ensure your potential candidates feel supported on the leadership track.

Successfully Transitioning

Succession is a period of significant change, and both the outgoing and the incoming leaders, as well as their teams, need to adapt to the changes.

In a transition period, outgoing leaders must plan for obsolescence: no regrets, and no vacuum left behind when you leave your position. Your successor will need mentorship and support so that they feel confident in taking over your position, and so your team is confident in their new leader. At this time, extract yourself from your prior role.

Incoming leaders will need support as they navigate the learning curve of their new position. Outgoing leaders must be the sounding board for their successor, challenge them, accelerate their learning, and support their relationships and decisions. Ensure the team is supported after the previous leader leaves, a few months into the transition, and as the new leader establishes new norms and a new direction for the team.

Succession works best when leaders prepare for the transition well in advance. If you are thinking about starting your own succession plan, think of the things you can start now, such as identifying potential successors and focusing on development. You and your organization will be on the best path to prepare for change.

HOW TO BE AN EFFECTIVE SUCCESSOR

Congratulations! It has been announced that you will succeed a senior leader in your company. Ideally, you have time between now and the day that you assume your new role.

In Passing The Torch, I suggested that the ideal transition period for outgoing leaders is one year from their planned exit. Even if you're lucky enough to have a full year before taking on your new position, there are challenges to being a successor. Here's how you can best use this transition period.

The First Six Months

The biggest thing you should do throughout this year is to spend lots of time listening to understand.

As soon as your new role is announced, meet with your current team to discuss the news and your new team to begin building important relationships. Be sure to arrange these meetings only after the change has been formally announced so that you are not burdening anyone with the knowledge before it is appropriate.

If you are succeeding an executive, chances are you are a senior leader and you will also need a successor. Identify your successor and create a transition plan to bring them into your current role and for you to extract yourself so that you can move into your new role. If you have less than a full year to prepare for your new position, I recommend extracting yourself from your previous role as quickly as possible.

On a personal level, you should also assess your own vulnerabilities. Whether it's gaps in knowledge or soft skills, or even finding out what it is you don't know, what do you need to learn as you move into your new role?

Within the first three to six months, you should begin transitioning your relationships to your successor and foster the relationships for your new role. Your current day-to-day tasks should be taken over by your successor at this point. Delegate projects to your successor, and take on projects from your new role.

The Next Six Months

At this point, you should fully transition out of your old position and into your new one. Mentor your successor to ensure that they can take on all of your responsibilities. This is also a critical time to seek mentorship from the person you are replacing, and transition their relationships to you.

Get to know the issues that you may face and start considering the long-term strategic plan. Train with the leader you are succeeding on any reports, budgets, and other technical business functions of the role. Work with the current leader to understand the exact scope of their role. Create a plan to fully transition into the role with 60-90 days prior to their exit and find projects that they can work on to be a mentor by your side as you take on the full role.

Most importantly, don't make changes just yet. In fact, by this point, you should have a good feel for the culture of the team and should be able to recognize when changes would be welcome. You haven't necessarily been hired to keep things status quo, but this is a period of major change for many people involved, not just you and the outgoing leader. There is tact in timing, and it's crucial to keep this in mind moving forward.

What if the outgoing leader was a beloved figure?

If you are replacing an executive, there's a good chance that they have been at the organization for a long time and are revered by their employees and peers. Acknowledge the legacy of the leader you're replacing. Your team may even feel loss at the departure of the previous leader. Give people time to grieve and encourage them to talk to you about your predecessor. You are a different person, of course, and will not lead the team exactly as the previous executive did, nor should you. Listen to understand what that leader did that worked so well, but don't try to be exactly like them. Learn from what they share with you.

What if they left under bad circumstances?

Regardless of the circumstances, be careful not to deprecate the work of the previous leader. It is important to acknowledge the work accomplished to this point by the previous leader and their team.

If your predecessor left on bad terms, make it clear that things won't magically transform overnight. Even if you are seen as the great white knight, everyone goes through the change curve. Desired change is no different and might even be harder because people expect a smoother transition. There may be a honeymoon phase, but it won't last forever.

One organization I worked with promoted a beloved CFO to CEO. The staff expected great things from the CFO, and for the first year, there was a honeymoon phase, but then it became clear that the CFO wasn't really up to being CEO. It wasn't the role they imagined. Manage everyone's expectations, including your own, and recognize that there's work left to do for both you and your team.

The First Three Months In Your New Role

Once you have officially started in your new role, you need to set your long-term goals with your team and the organization. What are you going to do now that you have ownership? It may not be possible to establish these standards while the previous leader still holds their title (out of respect during the transition period), but now it's time to make the role your own.

The timeframe right after this transitory year is also a critical period for you as a leader when you are firmly in your new position. But if you have set the foundation beforehand, you should be well-equipped to face anything your new role brings.

WHY A 360-DEGREE ASSESSMENT ISN'T ENOUGH FOR BUILDING STRONG LEADERS

Strong leaders aren't born. They're individuals who continually open themselves up for constructive critique for their growth and improvement. Great leaders are those who raise their self-awareness in order to be proactive in developing their future and the future of their team.

But how do they do this?

I've found that when paired with an action plan, a 360-degree assessment can transform not just a leader but their entire organization, creating the foundation on which everything is built.

As a leader, your 360 is a confidential survey primarily taken by your managers, direct reports, peers and other key stakeholders. When completed, the results highlight your leadership capabilities, focusing on skills such as people management, task management, execution abilities, communication and so on. It provides a full view of what core areas—strengths and weaknesses—you need to develop to be a more effective leader.

It's Not A Magic Bullet

While 360s provide great insights, they are not magic bullets that suddenly transform how you lead.

In order for real change through a 360, you have to be willing to critically look at yourself. I often coach leaders who think they're going to simply receive a list of tactical things to do to change. However, many are surprised by the personal work required for real, long-term leadership development.

For most people, you create your success by applying your strengths to react to the challenges of the day. But when you move into a leadership role, you are then responsible for developing others and creating for tomorrow. You must now learn how to apply your strengths in a more proactive rather than reactive way. This is the challenge I see when working with leaders, as this requires self-awareness, vulnerability, and support *with* a plan, not just a list of strengths and weaknesses.

So what does this mean? One completes a 360, receives their results, then what?

The Missing Link

Unfortunately, there is the danger that completing a 360 can cause more damage than good. This is determined by what is done with the assessment *after* all results are received.

What I've come across is that if you just do a 360 and don't develop a strategic plan that ties the results to your goals, all you are doing is highlighting your "faults." This doesn't offer solutions for how to be better in certain areas or how to use your strengths in a new way. Yes, it's important to understand where there are gaps in your skills, but it's just as important to build your confidence as a leader so you can be more effective. Developing a measurable action plan is part of this.

This plan must be created and implemented around what strengths you have, where you have certain gaps, and where you actually need to develop in relation to your and your organization's goals.

Creating An Action Plan

How do you actually build this plan?

Reflecting on the results of the 360, you can reframe their context in relation to the objectives for change/growth you've outlined. This allows you to look at your role in a new light, identify what types of skills are required to support specific results, which may include adding someone who has complementary skills that you "lack," and find innovative ways to bring about long-lasting, effective change. To build an effective plan, you must know who you are, where you're going, and what you need to do to get there. Plans are specific to your strengths, motivators and communication style.

A great example of a 360 being leveraged effectively comes from one of my clients, a senior leader in a chemicals manufacturing organization. In an environment with a number of safety hazards, her top priority was to keep her team safe. As such, she would often come across as aggressive when honing in on no-nonsense safety risks. When she received the results of her 360, she wasn't surprised that "assertive" and "lack of empathy" were highlighted as downfalls by her team. However, while her team knew her top priority was their safety, it was the way she talked to them that hindered and demotivated them.

Once identified this, we created a plan that played to her assertive strength but reframed how she conveyed her message, while actively listening to her team's feedback, closing her gap in empathy. Since then, she's moved forward in her position because she's more effective in her communication style in a way that is still authentic to who she is but acknowledges how her team hears her. Without having completed the 360, she wouldn't have known why her team was underperforming or not being receptive to her guidance, and we wouldn't have built an effective plan for her and her team's growth.

The End Goal

Ultimately, 360s are about bringing your strengths and your people to the next level, not a summary of pros and cons. Recognizing where and how you can be more effective, and then implementing strategies to become so, will see you transform from a good leader to a great leader.

FOUR SKILLSETS YOU CAN ALWAYS WORK ON TO IMPROVE AS A LEADER

The post-summer return to work feels like a chance to reset and keep improving upon ourselves. As an executive coach, I believe that there are always opportunities to learn something new. Leaders must not get complacent and be at a point where they think they know everything. I work directly with leaders and senior executives to help them build up their leadership skills, and there are four areas in particular that leaders can always keep working.

Develop a growth mindset.

People ask me all the time whether you are simply born a leader, or if you can become one. My answer is that anyone can learn and work to become a leader. Professor of Psychology at Stanford University Dr. Carol Dweck, wrote the book *Mindset*, which is centered around the idea of a *growth* mindset versus a *fixed* mindset. To me, this idea is groundbreaking for leadership. A fixed mindset is saying, "I can't do that," whereas a growth mindset is saying, "I can't do that yet, but I can learn."

Courageous leaders have growth mindsets because they willingly accept that they cannot always control what happens.

A fixed mindset is limiting in two very different ways: Some people might come from experiences where they think they are not good enough to do something, so they will not try. This is shaming talk, and it makes you stop before you can even begin. Other people might engage in defensive talk by saying, "How dare you, I am good enough," when they encounter obstacles.

To develop a growth mindset, assess every situation and tell yourself, "I can learn," or ask, "What can I do better next time?"

Set a healthy company culture.

Strong leaders often have enviable teams. From the outside looking in, it appears that these leaders have created company cultures that make others want to be part of what they are doing. If you are a senior executive or human resources leader looking to develop the culture within your organization, there are always actions you can take to build and enhance your own team or organizational cultures.

Building a culture takes intentional and thoughtful work. Being clear on your own values is a great foundational step from which you can work outward. In *The Culture Code*, author Daniel Coyle takes "culture" from being an identity to something you do. These behaviors are not always obvious at first glance, but they are critical in establishing relationships across teams.

To actively create your own company's culture, you must first build safety, share vulnerability and establish purpose. The key to building all three is empathy; leading with empathy will help your teams feel safe to accept feedback and have tough conversations, and they'll allow themselves to be vulnerable when they see you lead by example. These steps, in turn, will help your team drive toward a common purpose.

Based on this, ask yourself as a leader, what am I doing to make my team enviable?

Set and enforce your boundaries.

One of the challenges many of the leaders I work with face is establishing boundaries with their teams while still being available to support them. Others struggle with setting boundaries with senior leaders while being respectful, responsive and avoiding burnout.

Some also struggle to maintain boundaries with themselves so that they are fulfilled by a passionate career and can also spend time recharging and engaging with the people and personal activities they love. I often hear from leaders that they struggle with the feeling that they have no choice in their work. They say, "I have to be available to [insert any of the above] all the time." This is why it's critical to set boundaries.

When a leader does not enforce boundaries, it can affect their personal lives because they have to sacrifice one thing for the other. It also sets a precedent at work for behaviors that can spread across their team members. Recognize that every "yes" requires a "no," and ask yourself, "Am I saying, 'No,' to things that matter deeply to me, besides my career?" I constantly reinforce that leaders who set boundaries and take time for themselves show their employees that it's good to do the same. Set aside time for vacation, self-care and side-projects that you care about, and encourage your teams to make time for the things outside of work that matter to them.

Be creative, not reactive

I incorporate The Leadership Circle assessments into my work. This is an assessment that looks at if you practice creative versus reactive leadership, and it is a concept I always talk about with my clients. If you are choosing one side, you are actively rejecting the other.

Executives must work on their awareness of the two sides of leadership. I completed The Leadership Circle Profile for the first time a few years ago, and I found that the line between these two leadership styles is vulnerability: being able to accept uncertainty, risk and emotional exposure. The more you can let go of your desire to win and your need for approval, the more you can develop your skills as a creative leader. Stepping into creative and strategic leadership involves vulnerability. I continue to work toward being a more creative (or proactive) leader myself and with my clients.

The 15 Commitments of Conscious Leadership by Jim Dethmer, Diana Chapman and Kaley Warner Klemp is another resource that illustrates the two sides of leadership because it shows that every decision is made actively. Life happens by you, not to you. When you learn this, I believe you can begin to shift your perspectives—which is transformative for any leader.

The end of summer and the beginning of fall seems to be a particularly inspired time in the corporate world. You hopefully come back feeling rested and recharged, ready to put your foot on the gas on the next project or initiative. Take this attitude and apply it to your personal leadership goals.

CULTURE

If you are lucky enough to be someone's employer,
then you have a moral obligation to make sure
people do look forward to coming to work in the morning.

~ John Mackey

How do you prioritize people? Prioritizing people begins with getting clear on culture and relentlessly safeguarding it. Culture is the set of social norms of behaviour beyond how you do your work, and extends to how you treat yourself, each other, and every person you and your organization interact with. It pervades how you made decisions in what you say yes to as much as what you say no to. It even shapes your strategic priorities and direction.

Start with defining your company culture, including your values and behaviours that represent those values. Be willing to take a stand for your values – which begins in creating them. If your team or organizational values would please everyone and anyone, they might not be clear enough. Include how you show up, how you celebrate, how you navigate missteps, and how you'll deal with situations where someone has stepped on cultural norms; after all, we're all human and we make mistakes.

Consider each of your stakeholders as a customer, including your peers, your boss, and your direct reports. Enter relationships gradually to get to know the other person, whether it's a new hire or a new business partner, but take swift action when cultural norms are violated to repair and reset the relationship or move on if it's determined there wasn't a cultural fit after all.

As a leader, your role is to be the steward of the culture by modelling it yourself in the hardest moments including acquisitions, mergers, working through change, integrating new talent, making tough decisions, and giving and receiving feedback. When you model and safeguard a bold set of values, you'll attract the right people and they'll love coming to work.

HOW TO BUILD A TRUE FOLLOWING
AS A LEADER

L eadership is hard enough. Why make it harder trying to be all things to all people, hustling to be someone you're not?

In reading Dr. Brené Brown's book, *Braving the Wilderness: The Quest for True Belonging and the Courage to Stand Alone*, my mind went to my clients and when they lead with their authentic leadership style. I'm always amazed by the freedom many of them feel when they let go of who they "should" be and show up as they are, creating a greater sense of belonging with their team.

But, how can you be brave as a leader when standing out can feel so lonely and isolating? It sounds a little flippant, but you start by looking inward.

Connect To Your Goals And Values

Clearly defining and then connecting to your broader goals and values is crucial for honest leading. You gain a deeper understanding of what your greater purpose is, both personally and with your team. This gives you better clarity on where you're going, why this is important to you and how you will get there. Then, you can clearly share this with your team. You bet it's vulnerable, but this allows for more buy-in to create a more honest following.

Take A Value Stand

With clarity around your goals and values, you're better able to define your boundaries of what you are and are not OK with, particularly in relation to your values. It may be difficult at first as you begin to firm set boundaries, but practice makes better (not perfect – never perfect).

It takes courage to speak up, particularly if you disagree with someone else's point. So long as you say your piece, why you disagree, and do so in a respectful manner, you'll create a more connected and communicative dynamic. By having the courage to speak your honest mind, you support an environment that encourages conversation to grow with everyone's strengths.

The point here is that you don't have to make people shift their opinions if you disagree. You just have to give them your honest opinion, so they have different perspectives to make more informed decisions. This is providing real support and leadership.

Listen To Feedback

Just as it's important that you provide honest feedback, it's important you listen to feedback. Solicit feedback, and listen wholeheartedly. Hear if how you're authentic (or not) is alienating people and how to incorporate their feedback, so you can see more of the impact you want.

What I want to make clear is that "authenticity" is not an excuse for bad behavior. It's a fine line sometimes between not being a jerk, but having the courage to say, "I disagree, but will go with the group decision because I respect them." Say your piece and move on, regardless of the decision.

Allow Others To Discover Their Authenticity

What many clients share is that they find it hard to "fit in." As a leader, you can't. You can, however, belong because of your insights, thoughts, values, and so on. By showing up as your authentic self, you encourage others to do so. You help to foster an environment built on listening, working with individual strengths and supporting people as they authentically grow.

As a leader, you are on a relentless pursuit of personal development, demonstrating ownership and accountability for yourself. This action will inspire others to take ownership of their work and personal development as well. It's what honest leadership creates.

Nurturing Your Leadership Style

Connecting with your authenticity is great, but how can you nurture and grow your authentic style? A few things leaders who belong (but certainly do not fit in) have in common include:

- **A commitment to lifelong development:** No matter how "expert" they are, inspirational leaders are those who know there is always room for improvement, even if by 1%! This is about knowing yourself better as you change, connecting with your goals and values, and gaining insight into your purpose. The hardest thing to overcome is that you can't be who you were last year because everything changes – relationships, roles, markets, team members. Change is constant, and leaders who personally develop are more likely to successfully adapt.

- **High self-management:** Authentic leaders are thoughtful about what they say because they want to have intentional impact. They frame their thoughts in a way that connects with the individual, which requires a high level of empathy to adapt their style (not their character) in how they say something. The "how" is the intentional thought for impact.

- **Reflection for purpose discovery:** It's OK to look backward to move yourself forward. Understanding who you were then, who you are now, and how this connects to your leadership style is important for you to create a positive impact. In doing this, you build a stronger connection to your purpose, supporting yourself as you shift your leadership approach, so you can grow without abandoning your values, conviction, or character.

Leadership development is not about becoming comfortable as a leader. It's about stepping into discomfort time and again, knowing you'll be fine on the other side, whether victory or defeat, because of your authenticity and character. It's this courage to stand alone, as your purposeful self, to grow your honest following. Plain and simple, the world doesn't need more bland vanilla pudding; it needs your courage.

HOW TO BE A CHAMPION FOR WOMEN IN LEADERSHIP

The cause of gender equality in the corporate world has gained momentum. Women's leadership and mentorship groups are increasing. Women are becoming better represented in front-line and mid-management roles. However, I'm not sure that I've seen an increase in women leading in executive roles just yet.

I'm an advocate for both men and women in leadership. I remember being with my daughter a few years ago at a National Geographic Live speaker event with a woman marine biologist. When the scientist showed a picture of herself on a ship with over 15 men and no other women, my daughter leaned over and said, "Do you think I could do that one day?" It reinforced to me that if you can't see it, it's hard to believe you can be it, whether in the science field, leadership or anything else.

As a leadership and executive coach, I focus heavily on equipping individuals with the skills and mindset they need to be effective in a leadership role. Promotions into executive roles take candidates' career experiences as well as their well-roundedness as leaders into account. These candidates are usually in the mid-to-senior phases of their careers.

What we do not take into consideration is that women may also step out of the workforce temporarily around this time if they are choosing to grow their families. Not every woman has the same experience, but the reality is that often women take on much of the child-rearing responsibilities, especially early in a child's life. This has a significant impact on the decisions women make for their career and the opportunities they're offered, as a result.

What can we do from a societal and a business perspective to acknowledge this?

Remove Barriers In Organizational Structure

We must look at different approaches to the roles that we all play in and out of the workplace. Supporting both men and women to be on track toward leadership and, eventually, executive roles requires organizational changes to understand needs and identify barriers that keep an individual from putting his or her hand up.

Provide Opportunities To Develop Diverse Experience

Executives become well-rounded leaders because they are given the opportunities to grow their skill sets earlier in their careers. Companies must give men and women equal opportunity for exposure and development to be ready to step into executive roles.

A common misconception is that you need to specialize or narrow your focus earlier in your career in order to become an executive in your field. While knowledge in your specialty is important, diversity in experience is an asset in an executive role. Someone who wants to one day become an executive should expose themselves to as many business areas as he or she can. An awareness of the bigger picture can empower you to put your hand up for a senior leadership role. This means it is up to us, as leaders and peers, to provide our colleagues with ample exposure to different learning opportunities.

Be Wary Of Biases

Organizations must also address the unconscious systemic biases working against the upward mobility of women. I once worked with a woman executive who was taking over for a retiring male vice president. As she presented at a meeting in which they transitioned their roles, the attendees directed their questions to him and not her, which he answered.

It was not until after the meeting that she expressed how this action undermined her credibility, and he realized the impact that he made by innocently fielding the questions instead of deferring to her.

Women Leaders: Set Yourself Up For Success

Life as an executive can be demanding for anyone, and it can get lonely. Women, in particular, tend to "buck up" in these roles, feeling like they have much more to prove as an executive. They may either end up becoming too much of a people pleaser and not stand up for themselves, or overcorrect and are then perceived as aggressive.

Here is some advice I can give in this instance:

- Surround yourself with a diverse set of mentors and peers, both men and women. Have a personal organizational chart or "board of advisors" of mentors, peers and supporters in various aspects of your life. From there, identify gaps, if any.

- Learn to have hard conversations, balancing directness and empathy.

- Create and reinforce strong boundaries for yourself and your team, including time management.

- Develop your critical thinking and systems awareness through exposure to as many business areas as you can.

- Build your personal resilience to step into difficult situations.

- Hire an executive assistant if your role allows it and be willing to embrace other forms of support, too.

It gets political, and it gets messy. That's just leadership. Learn to let it roll off you rather than consume you. The most important advice I can give is to not base your identity on your executive role. We all have lives outside of work, and those parts of our identity are just as, if not more, important than our careers. Setting boundaries for yourself is crucial here.

One of my favorite stories on this is from former PepsiCo chairman and CEO Indra Nooyi. The day she was promoted to president, she came home to her mother who asked her to go out and buy milk before learning of the news. No matter our accomplishments, when we go home, we leave that part of our lives "in the garage," as she said.

In the blog post she wrote telling this story, Nooyi said: "Now, I'll admit, I've found it's rarely possible to be the kind of mother, wife, employee and person you want to be — all at the same time. Often, you need to make a choice, and that's especially true if you want to be CEO. There's no way around it." We must work to ensure that we are empowering both women and men to be able to make these choices.

HOW TO ENCOURAGE AND GROW A POSITIVE CULTURE THROUGHOUT YOUR ORGANIZATION

In the early days of companies, there is often a sense of camaraderie and shared purpose that employees might attribute to company culture. Establishing and growing intentional company culture is critical at this stage because it sets a precedent for how your company will operate moving forward.

When your team is on the smaller side, it seems much easier to establish company culture. But as the organization grows, how can you ensure your culture grows with you?

Defining Company Culture

First, we should think about what "company culture" is. I define culture as a collection of values, behaviors and expectations that show what your company stands for. In Four Skillsets You Can Always Work On To Improve As A Leader, I referenced the book *The Culture Code* by Daniel Coyle, where he distinguishes culture as something you do — not just your identity. Culture isn't a status you should aspire to; it should be something that you are already working on.

One example of company culture in action is at Boston University. According to Elizabeth McLeod, who reported on her observations of the university's culture in a 2012 *Fast Company* article, their employees hold campus citizenship to a high standard. Any employee walking across campus is encouraged to help anyone who looks like they might need help getting around.

This is a great example of bar-setting behavior that sets expectations which clearly shows what the company stands for and guides their employees' actions. It is very important to lead by example, but for culture to be successfully embedded in a company, policies need to be created and implemented to ensure that it continues to grow.

Building Policies Around Culture

I have found that there are cultural shifts when companies hit certain employee number milestones because leaders show resistance to add processes and policies related to company culture over time. They often feel that policies might lead to diminishing culture. I've seen this resistance occur at the 40-60 employee mark, then again at the 100-120 employee mark and so on. The resistance might come from hanging on to how good it was at the beginning, and a fear that putting policies in writing would risk losing that magic.

But as an organization grows, it can be difficult for team members to understand who does what. You don't know everyone as deeply as you do with a small team of 10 compared to growing to 100 and then 500 employees. And yet, the concept of "fit" becomes more important than ever for the company culture. Consistent behaviors that embody the company's values need to be continued.

Loss of consensus leads to confusions and assumptions, which could lead to conflict. Rather than assuming that everyone will be on the same page by just following other's leads, provide documentation and guidance around what is expected and how things are done.

For executives, it is critical to speak with your internal leaders and department heads about your company culture so they can implement it throughout the organization. Help them understand specific behaviors, actions and decisions that occur in their areas, and show them how to use values to guide how they do their work. Each team within the company might even have their own set of values in relation to the greater company values. As long as there is a shared understanding of the company values and support from executive leadership, policies can help create a shared understanding and, ultimately, company culture.

Naming Your Culture By Naming Your Values

Company values are quite commonplace. Most organizations have them written somewhere in their offices, maybe on walls or onboarding documents. But do you or your employees know what those values are? Conduct a self-audit as well as an audit of your leadership team. Do you know your company values? Can you say them without thinking? What are some of the ways you can be more consistent with your actions, behaviors and decisions to support those values?

Many organizations have values that are simply good, human values, such as honesty, trust and accountability. But shouldn't these already be expected from everyone in your organization? Instead, identify the values that make your organization different, not the ones others expect you to have. Be bold. Be willing to rub people the wrong way who don't share the organization's values. Watered down values mean nothing if you are not willing to take a stand.

Survey the organization, hold focus groups, have 1-to-1 conversations with people to understand what they think your company culture is and why, and the culture they believe the company ought to have and why. Great culture starts with an understanding of the company's purpose. Simon Sinek, author of *Start With Why*, has a famous TED Talk where he talked about Apple's culture, starting with their "why." "Think Different" means challenging the status quo, and this value is shared throughout the company.

For example, one of my company's values is "challenge." We uphold this value by only taking on clients who challenge us, and we challenge our clients to push beyond the norm and help make meaningful change. We're not afraid to turn down prospective clients who do not fit this value. At the same time, we only want to work alongside leadership coaches who share this value with us.

Once you have set your values, make sure you are also sharing them with your organization. As Daniel Coyle says in *The Culture Code*, be 10 times as clear about your priorities as you think you should be. Repeat your values — not just the essence. Your employees might come up with catchphrases or symbols. Even if you don't make them official, encourage these activities. Make it safe for your team to use them so they remember them, connect with the values and take it with them to their everyday thinking.

Getting your company culture to mean something to your organization entails defining what is important to you and then creating guidelines to ensure that your values grow with your company.

HIRE SLOW AND FIRE FAST: WHY LEADERS SHOULD HEED THIS ADVICE

"Hire slow and fire fast." If you are a senior leader, chances are you have heard this phrase before. Many leaders swear by it. Why has it become such a popular business saying?

What 'Hire Slow' Really Means

To hire slow means to hire with intention, not reaction. When you have a job to fill, you shouldn't simply replace the last employee who held the position or pull up an old job description template. Get really clear on what your needs and expectations are. Write a clear job description and define the skills and attributes required for long-term success, not just the immediate issues at hand.

Posting a job opening requires more consideration into business sustainability: long-term business success, succession, team dynamics and long-term role effectiveness, not just short-term projects and business needs.

Prepare to interview and assess the candidate beyond skills. Assess potential fit with the team, the leader and the organizational culture and values. Create a standardized interview to allow you to compare candidates fairly.

Speaking from my training and experience in HR, I also know that there are many kinds of biases that we can fall into during the hiring process. These biases can push us to hire a candidate who may end up not being a fit or to pass on the best candidate. Take your time, don't hire after just one or two interviews. Get perspectives from others in your organization, including peers, your leader or the team itself.

What 'Fire Fast' Really Means

To fire fast is to acknowledge that we're all human and make mistakes. But, we can have a bias toward giving someone ample forgiveness and time and hoping things will turn around. It's tough to make a call that things are not working and that it's time to part ways.

When you or the employee have made an error in the hiring process, firing fast means to confront the issue head-on and have difficult conversations. As I have said before, the ability to have tough conversations is essential for leaders. It takes courage and vulnerability for leaders to admit that they may have made a hiring mistake.

It is hard to make these decisions that will impact the organization negatively in the short-term, because you are going to be short-staffed again and will have spent time and money onboarding a new employee. But in the long-term, it is ultimately for the organization's benefit if the employee is not a fit.

Firing fast in a considerate manner means parting ways with the employee and giving them a soft landing to ease the transition because of the hiring fit error so that they can move on and find another job. Online retailer Zappos used to offer new employees a "quitting bonus," where new employees could receive $1,000 if they quit during their probation period. Amazon, which bought Zappos, adapted this policy and now offers employees $5,000 to quit. Employees can act accordingly with a cushion while they find their next role.

I'm not saying all organizations can (or should) do this, but it reinforces leaders' responsibility in taking action when a new hire isn't a fit, instead of waiting for them to quit.

What Is 'Slow' And What Is 'Fast?'

Both terms are relative to the organization. Hiring slow will depend on the organization's size and culture, and the sophistication of the hiring process. There is definitely such a thing as hiring too slow, trying to find the "perfect match," which doesn't exist. This leads to analysis paralysis, and we can become too fearful to hire.

Unless you're hiring for a seasonal or short-term position, consider what's at stake and the impact on the business. Are you committed to this person for 3-5 years? Have you thought clearly about how they will integrate with the team? Beyond immediate need for support, what workflow will this employee need to keep them engaged? This lack of careful consideration is common in organizations that hire too much too quickly, then end up having to let go of many employees at once because of a lack of fit.

What is "fast," exactly? When you think that you might have to fire someone, you must reflect on whether you have given this person enough runway into their new role. Organizations often have a probation period for new employees but do not actually assess fit during this probation period. Once you hire a new employee, how do you onboard them? How do you take this time to evaluate whether you've made a good decision? On the other hand, if you don't know for sure after three months, it's not a fit.

At first glance, "hire slow, fire fast" can come off harsh. However, in many ways, it gives both employers and potential employees opportunities to determine fit. We can look for the perfect match or the right answer, but right answers don't exist. Sometimes we hire too slowly out of fear of making errors. Or, we can be impatient with seeing results and let go of an employee who was a great fit, but to whom we didn't allow appropriate onboarding or enough runway to perform at the level required.

I think "hire slow, fire fast" appeals to leaders because it gives them some permission to slow down in a fast-paced, high-pressure world that pushes them to produce results as quickly as possible. Being reactive to business pressure and hiring fast can lead to long-term problems.

If you give yourself permission to hire slow, you can take the time you need to hire for the right fit. If you give yourself permission to fire fast, you are allowing yourself to be human and make mistakes. You are empowered to act quickly to avoid longer-lasting impacts on your business or on your hiring candidate.

LEADERSHIP IS A CUSTOMER SERVICE JOB—FOR YOUR TEAM AND BEYOND

In an organization, customer service roles are often delegated to the business development, marketing or sales departments. But when you are in a leadership role, you are also in a customer service role.

One common theme that I hear from the leaders that I work with is that they struggle to get buy-in for their ideas. "Why won't the executive team support my initiative?" "Why won't finance give us more budget for this?" "It's the right thing to do. Why won't they do it?" These leaders feel like they are constantly pushing uphill to get support.

A leader often thinks of themselves as an advocate for their team or their particular business unit. But a big part of advocating is providing a business case for an initiative, and simple advocacy doesn't work when the audience is tuned into WII-FM radio—"What's in it for me?" You need to sell your initiative to prospective customers.

Are you a leader? Then you're in customer service.

WII-FM just happens to be key to a salesperson's arsenal. Every salesperson knows that, in order to sell, you need to be able to convey that the benefits of what you're selling are important to the people you're selling to. It doesn't matter whether the solution has cutting-edge specs or that your project is altruistic. You need to help your audience see what's in it for them.

Within an organization, everyone is in sales. The question is: Who is your customer? For human resources, it's the employee. For finance, it's the budget. For IT, it's a solution or a vendor. However, when you advocate for one cause, you may see it as your only customer, which means you're losing sight of your other customers: everybody else.

By viewing other people within your organization as your other customers, you can reframe how you are trying to gain their influence and buy-in. Think about it this way: Have you been on the other end of a sales call where someone keeps trying to sell you something that you don't even want or need? Good customer service means meeting your customers' needs.

In the same way, leaders need to be able to put themselves in their customers' shoes. What are their pain points, and how can your solution address them? For example, if you are an HR leader trying to launch a new initiative, telling the executive team that they need to approve the project because "it's the right thing to do" may not be enough. Instead, tie it back to the strategic goals of the organization. If the company is trying to achieve a sales milestone, your HR initiative might help boost employee morale, which helps reduce employee turnover and increase productivity.

Here's the key to getting buy-in from prospective customers:

If you feel like you are struggling to get support for a project within your company, try thinking about each audience as your customer and how you can influence them to see the benefits of your initiative.

There are two possible ways that leaders might be falling short on their sales skills, especially toward executives or senior leaders. Technically focused leaders may get caught up in the features of the solution they are trying to get and forget to highlight benefits that will interest the leadership team. On the other hand, relationship-focused leaders may be spending so much time on achieving a resolution between their department and senior leadership that they struggle to ask for support or buy-in for their project.

To be an effective salesperson, you need two things: empathy and assertiveness. When you practice empathy, you can begin to understand what it is your audience cares about. People make decisions based on what's important to them. For some senior leaders, the benefits to the collective is enough. But for others, you may have to reframe the benefits in order to make connections with their priorities and what they care about. Assertive salespeople ask for the sale. This part might seem too simple and may be uncomfortable, but some leaders aren't direct about asking for what they need: a decision.

If you have worked to become more empathetic and more assertive and you're still not getting buy-in for your project, it's possible that you may need to rethink your solution. Some products or ideas need to be refined before they are ready, and leaders need to be prepared for this outcome.

Everyone in your organization is your customer.

Adopting a customer mindset even within our own organizations means considering leadership peers as our clients, which also helps round out systems thinking. Viewing the organization and analyzing the workings of the organization as a whole is a critical leadership skill.

Whenever you work on a project, ask yourself: Who are my customers? Who do I need to say yes to my initiative? That second question is a good reminder that you always have multiple customers. Look upward and across your organization for those customers. Once you determine your customer groups, you can create a better strategy to get the buy-in that you need.

When you apply customer service skills to your work, you can begin to think further about how you can serve all stakeholders, not just one. What's in it for me, for them, for the organization and for what we all care about? Am I talking to employees enough? What about other customer groups—am I getting to know their interests and pain points? Am I appealing to their priorities?

Trying to get buy-in for your project from your senior leaders or your leadership peers? Change your thinking from an "us vs. them" model to "what are they looking for and how can I get there?" If you can't influence them to buy your idea, then perhaps you haven't helped them see the features and benefits of the idea you're selling. The next time you work on a new project or initiative, remember to think of all of your stakeholders as customers.

SUCCESSFUL ACQUISITIONS CARE ABOUT CULTURE

Mergers and acquisitions are major events that bring change to every part of both organizations involved. These integrations need to be done smoothly, with the expectation that business operates as usual for clients. Company leaders often form transition groups that focus on operational aspects, driven from a strategic or financial perspective. However, two important aspects for the long-term success of the merger or acquisition process should be handled with just as much care: people and culture.

Getting acquired is often received as a mix of both a positive and negative business event. Up to this point, your company has accomplished significant achievements, and another organization has recognized that. It also brings uncertainty, shifts in responsibility, and new people, ideas and behaviors. Even breaking the news to employees that your organization is getting acquired needs to be done with much consideration.

Prioritizing People Right From The Start

From an employee's perspective, a merger or acquisition naturally brings some trepidation. They do not know if their jobs will be made redundant. They will likely lose some colleagues. They do not know if their compensation will be affected. They may feel uncertain about starting over with new teammates and new leaders.

Drama and stories can take over without clarity in communication from leaders, or early support by leadership, especially a senior HR leader. Those being acquired can feel like they are not important, that the work done to this point is being erased and being taken over by the new entity that is "better." It is important to acknowledge what they have done to this point was essential to success and that it might look different going forward together to achieve the next level of success.

It is also critical to ensure that a strategic people leader has a seat at the table as early as possible in the transition period. This step is often overlooked or comes after the acquisition. Considering the integration of people is critical to a successful merger or acquisition, a chief people officer or senior HR leader will bring the strategic people perspective to the table as early as the dealmaking stage while the other leaders focus on operational, financial and technology leadership.

Acknowledging Change With Employees

Even employees who are excited about the merger go through the change curve. There is initial excitement in the honeymoon period and then the organization still goes through the change dip.

Leaders need to help their teams turn the page on their old identity and develop a new future with an adapted identity. This means spending time acknowledging what was great about the past and what will be missed; what maybe wasn't so great about the past and what won't be missed; what needs to be honored or grieved to be able to move forward. This is an exercise that I have taken many teams through.

I recently started working with the leadership team of an organization that is in the early stages of an integration, and they engaged my services even before the closing date of their merger. Not only have they thought about the integration of the two workforces, they have also begun to consider the implications of the merger on talent development and restructured their succession pipeline. A merger disrupts previous succession plans. If you want to hold on to the individuals in your organization, you need to nurture them throughout the process. Consider bringing in coaches, change consultants and other external support as needed to supplement the internal leadership team.

Starting Over Together

Merging two organizations is not as simple as consolidating teams or shifting departments. Leadership teams create plans for the newly integrated organization, as mergers and acquisitions often require us to rethink our goals based on the new capabilities, vision and structure of the organization. The key to moving forward together is alignment to those organizational goals, not just team or individual goals.

Psychologist Bruce Tuckman developed a model for group development, where teams go through four phases: forming, storming, norming and performing. This model also applies after a merger. Newly merged teams go through the same process:

- Forming: Determining what your goals are

- Storming: Looking at how to work together to reach those goals

- Norming: Making decisions toward those goals

- Performing: Acting on the decisions that were made to reach the goals

This process is important for being able to move forward and create a new company culture — and parts of culture live in every element. Poor integrations can happen when any one of these steps gets skipped, especially forming. To get alignment on company goals, leaders need to articulate what they are and ensure that they are understood throughout the organization.

Integration Isn't Business As Usual

Once the merger closes, senior leaders must dedicate time to support the integration of people during the transition period. Executive teams need to take a step back and accept that short-term results may be lower during this time, in the interest of ensuring better long-term outcomes. Take this time to listen, consider and explore, with thoughtful communication and listening.

The transition period can also be taxing on leaders throughout the organization who are on the front lines, who are dealing with emergent issues, smoothing out feelings of uncertainty and implementing the changes set out by the executive team. Leaders can burn out because there is so much work to do all throughout, from the lead up to the closing and for some time after the merger. Senior leaders need to be mindful of what they can do to provide support throughout the organization.

Paying attention to company culture matters during integration — as does being intentional about creating a new culture together. Without talking about culture, people don't just shift and change. You have to talk about it a lot, before, during and well after a merger. And then, when ready, you can explore what is possible for the future together that neither entity could have achieved apart.

STRATEGY

The essence of strategy is choosing what not to do.

~ Michael Porter

The heart of strategy begins with envisioning a future that doesn't yet exist and is uncertain to even be achieved. To get clear on the future, tell the story about where you want to be, including what you want, not what you *don't* want. Surprisingly, this can be difficult to discern and requires engaging in regular reflection, looking backwards for learning to support looking ahead. It also requires courage to articulate and write down possible futures and tests to identify the future you want to move towards. This process is much like choosing a destination when sailing a ship to somewhere you've never been before and have limited information about the destination. One must be decisive or else find themselves going in circles or where the wind randomly blows.

On the way to reaching your vision for the future, consider long-term implications of decisions and focus on effectiveness over efficiency to ensure sustainability on the path. Celebrate and reflect on both successes and lessons learned to maintain energy and develop new capabilities for the ambitious journey that lay ahead.

When it comes to actual written strategic plans, keep them concise and priority focused. That means your top three priorities, not top 30. Create a clear line to show how these top priorities will get you to your desired future.

Finally, never create or work through your strategy in a vacuum; ensure you build a diverse leadership team and actively seek varied and conflicting perspectives to inform and challenge your thinking.

DIVERSITY ISN'T AN OUTCOME; IT'S A STRATEGY FOR BUSINESS SUCCESS

Most companies have historically viewed diversity as an issue: "We lack it, so we need to have it." The solutions become reactionary. They may feel that they are missing women from their leadership team, so they add one. Or, they bring in an individual from a visible minority group to essentially fill a quota. But diversity should not be treated as a project outside of your core business operations. When done well, diversity *is* a business strategy and leads to better business outcomes.

Short-Term Crisis Versus Long-Term Strategy

I used to coach an executive whose organization had prepared a long-term diversity plan but shelved it when #MeToo came about. The same thing happened when the Black Lives Matter movement brought many to question the lack of diversity in major organizations. They pivoted to emergency thinking and responded to "crises," rather than moving the needle with any of the groups they wanted to include. Instead of staying the course with their plan, which welcomed diverse cultural, gender and ability perspectives, they were reacting and not getting traction, losing the bigger view of diversity in the organization.

To step away from the short-term, reactive thinking around diversity, you must broaden your sense of inclusivity so that you're not just "putting out fires" and addressing one group at a time. If you are constantly reacting, you end up moving from one fire to another, putting them out as they arise. Create a long-term strategy to increase the entirety of diversity in your organization. While you can still react to new blindspots that come to your attention, you want to stay the course of your overarching diversity strategy. Ask broader strategic questions about what you are creating, not just what you are cleaning up. What is the future workforce and future leadership you aspire to be as an organization five, 10 and 15 years from now? How does the organization that you would be proud to lead look, think and act? Challenge yourself to explore that vision and look at it through the lens of many different groups to create an informed, full picture.

Diverse Leadership Teams And Boards

Real diversity means that there is a great variety of perspectives, personalities and thinking in the organization. Diverse viewpoints bring greater critical thinking, systems thinking, strategic thinking, empathy, courage and innovation. When you view diversity as part of your greater business strategy, it becomes a tool to support your business outcomes. It is integral to effective critical thinking, especially in leadership teams. Otherwise, we are willfully blind to other ways of thinking and don't have enough to think about the future. This leads to blindspots—what we know is what we know, because we don't know any better. When we all think the same, we think our viewpoint is the only viewpoint. Diversity in thinking means less homogenous thinking, which means the ability to be courageous is reduced. Diverse workplaces demand the *different*: They create more humanity and empathy and create courageous culture.

Having a diverse board is a good start to driving diversity in your organization because the board provides perspectives that the senior leadership team members might not consider from their perspectives. Boards exist not only for oversight and to be the conscience of an organization but also to be the challengers of perspective and short-sighted thinking. They exist to expand the perspectives of the senior leadership and consider the longer-term from every angle.

Ensuring A Path To Diverse Leadership

It is one thing to have a diverse workforce and another to create a path for diverse leadership. Because we don't know what we don't know, we have to challenge how we view what a leader is. This shows up as a bias in how we interview and promote. Seek out overlooked or nontraditional strengths demonstrated by your team members. Learn about diverse cultures, genders, personalities and backgrounds to understand how strengths show up in different ways other than what you may be accustomed to. Nurture those strengths and go out of your way to give opportunities for growth to a wide range of people. Get really curious about how to develop leaders from different groups of people. Learn about those groups of people and what works to develop them, and also what they need to remove any barriers to development.

Creating a path for diverse leadership doesn't mean creating leadership initiatives for one group over another, because it can't be one group's turn over another. Create a "yes, and" culture of development. Continue to develop your employees and offer consistent development opportunities to new groups and individuals, but also be willing to adapt your idea of development to harness the greatness in different kinds of people. What works to develop strengths in one group may not be the right approach to develop another.

Diversity As A Business Strategy

To truly educate yourself and better understand what diversity means to you and your organization, go out and talk to a variety of groups within your stakeholders, your employees and your greater community. You can't just dream it up in isolation—you need input to inform your views, unlearn previous assumptions and develop new behaviors.

Diversity as a strategy also does not happen overnight or through a sprint of hiring decisions. In order for your organization to become truly diverse, the timeline is not months to a year—it takes several years to see results, so you have to stay the course. Get clear on why you are working toward diversity because it has to be tied to your business strategy.

Diverse leadership can be linked to greater performance. When diversity is aspirational and tied to your greater business strategy, you have a better chance of receiving buy-in from the organization because it reflects on your outcomes. Be proactive and start asking broader strategic questions today, and start building the foundation for a truly diverse organization that you can be proud of in the years to come.

HOW TO IMMEDIATELY IMPROVE
YOUR STRATEGIC PLAN

Have you looked at your strategic plan recently? Is it an actual business strategy, or is it merely a list of tactics to execute through the year ahead without a full understanding of where the organization is going?

Strategic execution of tactics, while important, is not a strategy in and of itself. Ultimately, your strategy should answer where your business is going (your vision for the three to five years ahead), along with outlining what the organization will say yes to and what it will say no to. This includes looking at customers, partners, employees, your approach and more.

If you're worried that outlining a longer-term picture of your company may limit the flexibility of your strategic execution, stop. Yes, you may have to change your execution over the course of the company's life. However, if you don't first have a clear understanding of where you're going, then any amount of execution won't have an impact, no matter how well it's planned.

Set a destination, but allow for flexibility along the way.

Concise Strategic Plans

While your strategic plan must include key information, it's not meant to be a long-winded writing exercise. Some of the most effective plans I've worked with and on are limited to one page.

By limiting your strategy to one page, you get your ideas on paper in a format where you can see all their interconnections. This allows you to consider the internal aspects of your business (the service and product) and the external aspects (your clients, potential clients and vendors), seeing where they're aligned and where there may be gaps.

In doing this, you keep yourself at a higher level of thinking without getting pulled down into the weeds. This means you identify the following when developing your strategy:

- Who your customers are

- What your clients' pain points are

- What value your company provides to relieve these pains

- How the business provides value to clients

- Who or what your key resources and partners are

- What your unique value proposition is

- The cost structure for making money

- What your company wants to be known for

Remember that you, as the leader, are tasked with building the strategy, not the strategic execution.

Actively Looking For Gaps

Having identified this top-down strategy, you can now determine what you're going to do to test it through experimentation, along with asking curious questions to elicit feedback. In other words, you're testing to determine if you're answering what your clients actually need or what you think they need. After all, you may execute well, but if no one is going where you are, you're not going to sell anything.

When you actively look to poke holes in your strategy, you gain clarity to see if you're:

- Attracting the right market

- Highlighting the right value for your audience

- Answering a real need

- Ignoring aspects of the market or client base

If you identify a gap, pivot and make changes to your overall strategy, not just in your execution of the strategy, as this will help you build a better strategic plan going forward.

What's important is that you test your strategy with people in the real world — your clients, potential customers, stakeholders, etc. — and not just a management consultant or internal leadership team. It's only after you've done this and identified where the gaps or misalignments are that you can get clear on your tactics, metrics and how you're going to move forward.

With this clarity in your strategy, you, along with your team, can build the strategic execution around how you're going to get to where you're going and why those are the tactics for your overall strategy.

Take a step back and ask yourself: Is your current strategic plan moving you forward to where you want to go and where your customers need you to go? If not, think about how to elevate it from a strategic execution plan to a strategic business model that aligns with your customers.

WHY REFLECTION IS CRUCIAL TO LEADERSHIP, FUTURE PLANNING AND SUCCESS

Whether it's the previous year ending or thinking about the year ahead, this time always seems to bring about a natural urge to reflect. You might have just come back from vacation, or a slowdown over the holidays, and enjoyed some quality time with your family (even if virtually this year). Now that you are back in the swing of things, you might be working on budget-setting or conducting interviews to determine bonuses.

A new year provides a time for some self-reflection, and I believe that reflection is just as important and beneficial for leaders to do themselves and with their teams.

Looking Back To Look Ahead

Reflection isn't just about reminiscing—it's also about taking stock of where you are now and where you want to be. It's difficult to project how you want to grow and develop without considering where you have come from. Reflecting on past performance gives you a foundation to plan for your future development. When planning for the future, individual and team reflection helps leadership teams integrate qualitative performance into their annual and long-term assessments, not just quantitative benchmarks.

Create a process for reflection. Leaders can reflect on their own and then share their findings with others in a strategy meeting, or you can set aside time during a planning meeting for each person to reflect. You can ask questions like, "Did we meet our goals, tangible and intangible?" Take some time to actually review your strategy documents and see how you're tracking progress. Boards, when conducting CEO performance reviews, should also look back on the past year to anticipate the year ahead.

Individual self-reflection is also important, giving leaders a chance to think back on the broader aspects of their leadership. As an executive or senior manager, look back on the relationships that you have cultivated at work, internally and externally. What part have you played in bringing people along? So many leaders focus on the growth and development of the people who report to them but forget about their own personal learning and development. What are your proactive learning goals? What do you want to learn and how do you want to learn it?

Envisioning The Future Through Storytelling

I've worked with leaders, leadership teams and boards on strategy planning and vision setting. The latter process always seems to be the most intimidating.

In these sessions, we do an exercise where they write a postcard from the future. Imagine you get to the end of the year and you report back to yourself today that it's been the best year. What is different about a year from now? What impact are you having? What has become easier? How will you know if you've been successful? Resist the urge to analyze and just tell the story of how you got there. This exercise takes the word "vision" away and helps to remove the intimidation factor.

You can do the same with a postcard from the past. Imagine you are sending yourself a postcard from a year ago. What was different about then? What was the impact you were making? What were you hoping would happen in the year ahead? Break it into quarters, months or any other "chapters" to help you tell the story in chunks. Look back on the vision that you set last year. Is this where you wanted to be a year ago? Any successes? How far have you progressed in a year? Storytelling is a fabulous way to engage in reflection.

The Value Of Reflecting On Success

Recently one of my clients, an executive from the construction industry, told me that his company just won a massive bid and is about to take on the actual construction work. The bid process had taken them 14 months from start to finish, so they had been working toward this point for a long time. Around 70-80 people were directly involved in the bid, but he later said that, when adding in contractors and tradespeople, the process involved close to 300 people.

This might be a normal occurrence in construction or similar industries, but it does not make the feat any less amazing. After reflecting on the process, my client realized that yes, it was worth celebrating and that it was important to reflect on what a great achievement it was for everyone involved. Think about it this way: Entire buildings could be constructed within 14 months. Where were they at when they submitted the bid? Where are they now?

Celebrating the win is great for morale and by acknowledging their role in helping to win this contract, he has provided serious motivation for his employees and contractors to get started. Now they have a ton of work to do, but it's worth looking at the finish line they just crossed before they look forward to the next one. Their next celebration will be recognizing the achievement of the first shovel in the ground.

Reflecting On Lessons Learned

When we don't take the time to reflect, we skip past the learning. We miss out on opportunities to find wisdom in future planning and can impair our own strategic planning. This past year holds especially significant learnings. For example, what did we learn about dealing with uncertainty? How will this year be better? Where are you at now? Where do you hope to be a year from now? What's changed?

We have to reflect on past performance to think about future development because it's otherwise hard to see the evolution in our story. Reflection doesn't have to take a long time. As a leader, you can devote as little as an hour of your time to the process. You can spend 10 minutes discussing your learnings at your next meeting with your team. Dedicating time and effort toward reflection only strengthens your future planning.

YOUR SHORT-TERM DECISIONS COULD UNINTENTIONALLY CREATE LONG-TERM PAIN

"Hope is not a strategy. We have to plan."- Dr. Julie Gerberding, former director of the Center for Disease Control

A client was faced with a problem employee, who also just happened to be the company's top salesperson. Under pressure to ensure his team met sales targets for the quarter, my client was hesitant to address the problem since they "needed" this employee for their team sales performance. After discussing why to either keep the employee and do nothing about the problems, let the employee go, or find a third option, along with considering the longer-term impacts of this short-term decision, my client came to a conclusion: Short-term decisions always have long-term impact.

Yet, the pressure to produce results with quick wins often overrides any connection between today's decisions and their long-term impacts. That's because a quick win shows you immediate results, whereas long-term impact is fairly nebulous without any concrete clarity of what the results could be. That said, while connecting your short-term decisions to its longer impact won't give you any guarantee of what will happen, it does give you the ability to see what your options could be, helping you to make a more sound decision in the short term.

How To Determine Long-Term Impact

Sometimes, a short-term decision may be more painful (terminate the problem employee, along with their potential sales) but will have the greater impact you want in the long term (more star salespeople, a supportive team, engaged employees).

Of course, simply considering the long-term impact doesn't mean you'll make a different short-term decision. It means that you are considering your options and whether your short-term thinking will create long-term stress. So, how do you start determining what the long-term stress will be?

- **Acknowledge** that it's human nature to want instant gratification, so the short-term win will make you feel good and relieve some of the pressure that might be on you, even if self-imposed. Then, give yourself permission to pause in the moment and think about the future. Notice your behavior and why you're feeling the way you are. This helps to move you to a place of real choice in your immediate decision by consideration for the greater impact.

- **Gather additional information,** as you can't know the actual outcome of a decision until after it's been made. In these cases, you need to pay attention to outside guidance, such as the wisdom and insights of others, as well as your internal gut instincts. Share the problem at hand and what decision you have to make, asking what future impacts they might foresee. This will help you gain clarity on whether the quick wins of today will take you closer to where you want to go.

Of course, how much consideration time you need is dependent on the scope and weight of the decision. In some cases, a short pause will do. In others, you'll need to seek outside guidance from multiple sources. Regardless, it all begins with considering the long-term impact on your overarching goal.

- **Consider** outside insights, along with what you want your team to be in relation to what your company's goals are. This gives you something more concrete to base a decision on than "long-term impact."

For example, my client had to ask what keeping his top sales performer, who was the only problem employee, would do for the short and the long term in relation to increasing their sales for the year — not just the quarter. Was it worth firing one star performer and potentially seeing your other staff grow, or keeping the employee and hoping that they change? (Don't worry, there were other options considered, but they all started by merely considering a step beyond the different options available.)

- **Decide and move forward.** The difference here is that you are now aware of the options and potential impact on you, your team and your company. The goal is not to dwell indefinitely to define certainty for the future. It's merely to consider your possibility to better inform your decisions of today.

Firing a star salesperson might feel uncomfortable, leaving one to immediately second guess themselves. Over time, though, the morale of the team picks up, people start communicating, and there are increased sales from all sales staff, which has them surpassing the yearly targets. Keeping a star salesperson might allow one to make the targets for the quarter, but the rest of the team turns over every three months and all other sales are below target for the rest of the year.

Without telling you what my client's decision was (it was the right one for the company), because of the pause he took to consider the different impacts and outcomes of his decision, his team flourished and he now has a healthy environment that fosters all employees.

Believing that short term and long term are separate entities is foolish. Your short-term decisions will always have some form of future impact. By considering the future, even for a minute, you give yourself the right options to move you closer to the impact that you want. Create the right domino effect by pausing to connect your decisions of today to the impact it has on where you are going.

EFFICIENCY IS JUST ONE PART OF AN EFFECTIVE LEADER'S TOOLKIT

Regardless of industry, efficiency is a major business goal. Efficiency is performing in the best possible way with minimal waste of time, effort and resources. Leaders aim to get the most out of what is put in. At first glance, efficiency might seem to be in conflict with effectiveness, which leaders also need in order to succeed. But the two are not at odds; in fact, efficiency is an element of effectiveness.

Effectiveness Vs. Efficiency

If efficiency is performing in the best possible way with minimal waste of time, effort and resources, effectiveness is accomplishing a purpose and producing the intended result. Being effective is about doing the right things while being efficient is about doing things right. Effectiveness is focusing on long-term impact, while efficiency is focusing on short-term goals.

Efficiency is task-oriented—focusing on productivity, meeting key performance indicators and submitting deliverables—all of which are important for any business. Processes and clarity around goal achievement is important to keeping teams on track and tracking their progress. These markers, such as sales and project completion, are often easy to track and report across teams and stakeholders. But a sole focus on efficiency can have the same effect as having blinders on. Efficiency for efficiency's sake, unmoored, can keep leaders from looking at the big picture.

Effectiveness takes a wider view, looking at today's activities and seeing if the long-term ripple effects are setting a positive foundation for the future. It's important to be doing things that are aligned with the strategic goals and vision of the company or team first and then focus on doing them well, in a way that leads to the desired outcome. Effectiveness may seem more difficult to assess, but leaders can track the progress of their strategic objectives through subjective key performance indicators such as measures of culture, employee engagement and organizational values.

A good way to gauge how your company fares in terms of efficiency and effectiveness is to analyze a common goal for many companies: reducing customer complaints. An efficiency-focused company may see success in simply addressing existing problems as they come. But thinking about effectiveness means listening to the client and finding opportunities to surprise and delight them, and going above and beyond to guarantee customers are happy, not just satisfied.

Focusing On Effectiveness, Sometimes At The Expense Of Efficiency

Effectiveness should always come first, but an efficiency lens can be applied to effectiveness. This is especially true for startup founders, for example, who need to drive efficiency to achieve traction early while planting seeds for future frameworks for growth. For them, efficiency is a focus at the start, but not in the long term.

For senior leaders and executives, in particular, there comes a time when a review of effectiveness calls for a pivot. Leaders have to be vulnerable and lean into inefficiency so that they can achieve long-term goals. Public companies that report quarterly sales, for example, may have to report losses for a certain period while they invest in new products, services or procedures that ultimately will improve their bottom line. Stakeholders may hold leaders accountable for those losses, and those leaders will then need to lead the organization through a tough time in order to be more effective in the long term.

Effective leaders work on important but not urgent tasks. This often requires more mindfulness amid the daily grind of endless tasks and fires that need to be put out but helps to set you up for future success. When looking toward the horizon, leaders should evaluate the organization's strategies to determine whether or not they are coming closer to their objectives. This requires studying the interconnectedness of your work with the work of others, internally and externally. Are we working on the right things? Sometimes, when you take this view, you may have to pivot your KPIs to keep moving in the right direction.

What Driving Effectiveness Looks Like

Leaders should also be pushing for effectiveness with their teams. Focusing on efficiency and simply getting things done hinders professional development. Are you just getting through your to-do list or are you setting your team up for future success? You can give an answer to an employee in 10 seconds several times a day for the next 10 years. Or, you can spend a few hours over the next few months to help that person learn and coach them in developing knowledge, confidence and autonomy so that you won't have to answer that kind of question again in the future.

Effectiveness also means sharing the *why* with employees, not just the *what*. Providing awareness and perspective on their work helps employees find purpose and motivation. It helps to spark creativity and opens up new ways of thinking and doing. Knowing what everyone is working toward leaves room for creative ideas that they may not have had otherwise. The next time you ask an employee to create a deck, for instance, let them know the intended impact, purpose and audience of the presentation. Is it for a board meeting? What are they deciding at the meeting, and what will they need to see to make a decision? Your team members may surprise you because they'll think about completing the task a little differently than if you had just told them what to do.

Leaders ultimately need to always look at the long-term vision for their teams and for the organization. If you focus on effectiveness, efficiency will come.

ABOUT INCITO

Incito is a premier leadership development firm that elevates executive and leadership team mindsets and creates hyper-effective, holistic leaders. Our clients experience a choiceful evolution of mindset that shifts their strengths and skills from the certain to the uncertain, allowing them to grow from reactive experts to strategic, future-focused leaders.

Incito goes beyond traditional leadership development and focuses on the executive or leadership team as a whole, helping leaders focus on what's truly important — both in and out of the workplace — so they become both personally and professionally fulfilled and can finally remove the unknown obstacles to reveal their leadership greatness. This is achieved through a highly custom, personalized approach that focuses on the leader as a whole so they can adjust ineffective, learned mindset and behavior patterns first, and then effectively evolve the best leadership skills and tactics second.

Incito's goal is to create leaders who have the confidence and mindset to create their highest and best outcomes, not only for themselves, but for their employees, teams and businesses.

To learn how Incito can help you and your company reach higher levels, visit www.incitoleadership.com/contact and schedule a call.

ABOUT JENN

Jenn Lofgren is a Master Certified Coach, speaker, author, avid contributor to the Forbes Coaches Council and a trusted partner for senior executives and growth organizations. She is CEO and Managing Partner of Incito, a premier leadership development firm that elevates executive and leadership team mindsets and creates hyper-effective, holistic leaders. When not inspiring leaders, Jenn volunteers with at risk youth and works to support the arts, business and the community. To learn more visit: www.incitoleadership.com

Made in United States
North Haven, CT
03 August 2022

22165625R00165